BRITISH POLITICS IN TRANSITION

Francis Boyd

BRITISH POLITICS
IN TRANSITION
1945–63

FREDERICK A. PRAEGER, *Publisher*
New York • London

FREDERICK A. PRAEGER, PUBLISHER
64 UNIVERSITY PLACE, NEW YORK 3, N.Y., U.S.A.
77-79 CHARLOTTE STREET, LONDON W.1, ENGLAND

Published in the United States of America in 1964
by Frederick A. Praeger, Inc., Publisher

Library of Congress Catalog Card Number: 64-16667
Printed in the United States of America

FOR
ELIZABETH, RACHEL and NICHOLAS

ACKNOWLEDGMENTS

I acknowledge with thanks the permission of the following publishers and authors to quote from the books and documents listed below: Hutchinson Publishing Group, London, *A State of England*, by Anthony Hartley; Director of Publications, Her Majesty's Stationery Office, *Hansard*; Hodder and Stoughton, London, and Houghton Mifflin, Boston, *Power and Influence*, by Lord Beveridge; Odhams Press, London, *Herbert Morrison, An Autobiography*, by Lord Morrison of Lambeth; Jonathan Cape, London, and Schocken Books, New York, *The Future of Socialism*, by C. A. R. Crosland; Cassell, London, and Houghton Mifflin, Boston, *The Second World War*, by Winston S. Churchill; George Allen and Unwin, London, *The Glory of Parliament*, by Harry Boardman; Conservative Central Office, *Official Report*, Blackpool Conference, 1962; Macmillan, London, *A Short History of the Labour Party*, by Henry Pelling; Macdonald, London, *The Labour Story*, by Emanuel Shinwell; Students' Representative Council, Edinburgh University, *In Praise of Politics*, by Jo Grimond; Parliamentary Profiles, *The Business Background of Members of Parliament*, by Andrew Roth.

CONTENTS

PART ONE

The Machinery of Politics: Motives, Parliament, Parties

PART TWO

Actions and Reactions

PART ONE

THE MACHINERY OF POLITICS:
MOTIVES, PARLIAMENT,
PARTIES

I

A PERIOD OF CHANGE

THE first world war caused a social and economic upheaval in Britain. The country's economic power had
already begun to decline before the war began, but the
effects of this, together with the changes which war-time
living had brought, were not widely recognised to have
altered British society permanently until the war was
over. The greatest single change made by the war was in
the status of women. Women had begun to campaign vio-
lently for the vote before the war, but the needs of the
war itself made work for women in munitions factories,
canteens, and in the armed forces as nurses, ambulance
drivers and so on.

   The Representation of the People Act, of February
1918, which gave the vote to all adult men, gave the vote
also to women over thirty years of age. The Sex Disquali-
fication (Removal) Act, of November in the same year,
permitted women to stand for election to Parliament, and
to take up civil appointments hitherto closed to them. At
the general election of 1918 six million women were
qualified to vote. The Representation of the People (Equal
Franchise) Act, 1928, gave women equal rights with men
in national and local elections. It gave the vote to seven
million more women—the under-thirties or "Flappers"
—and in the general election of 1929 there were over

fifteen million women voters, compared with thirteen-
and-a-half million men.

Great though these changes were, the results of the
second world war altered British society even more profoundly. The policy of full employment which successive
governments have applied in Britain since 1945, and the
maintenance of a high rate of taxation to finance expanding social services, have greatly reduced the extent of
poverty and have limited, though not stopped, the growth
of large individual incomes. While large private fortunes
have been accumulated since 1945, the general standard
of living has risen.

It was symbolic of this alteration that the Representation of the People Act, 1948, applied for the first time in
British parliamentary history the principle of "one man,
one vote" on the basis of adult suffrage. This Act
destroyed the privilege of plural voting which had been
enjoyed by a minority of the electorate—owners of business premises and university graduates—and abolished
the right of the City of London, the headquarters of
Britain's financial interests, to return two members to the
House of Commons with an electorate which was much
smaller than that of the average constituency. The effect
of this change can be shown vividly. At the general election of 1945, the City of London electorate was 10,830,
of whom 3,767 lived in the constituency and 6,608 had a
"business premises" vote. The rest of the voters at that
election were in the armed services. This small electorate
returned two members, neither of whom was, naturally
enough, a socialist. Penistone, an industrial area in the
West Riding of Yorkshire, had an electorate of 81,079,
including only one "business premises" voter. Penistone
returned one member—a Labour man.

This book will be concerned in the main with politics
since 1945. It will seek to isolate the factors which have
caused the larger political parties in Britain to seek new

positions in which the parties, while retaining their identities, could develop policies which modified or ran counter to the traditional views of their respective supporters. This process of adaptation still continues and cannot be abandoned if the party structure of British politics is to be preserved, and if the country's economy and society are to be equipped to give Britain a useful part in world affairs.

The chief agent of change has been the decline of Britain's power, both economic and military; and the chief task of the political parties has been to diagnose the situation accurately, to prescribe the correct treatment, and to present the new course to the public in a form intended to be as little disagreeable to national pride as possible. This has meant at times that the true nature of the changes imposed on Britain has been concealed. Indeed, it may be that in the pressure of day-to-day events the party leaders themselves have not always seen the final destination of a particular line of policy.

Anthony Hartley, in his book, *A State of England*,[1] wrote:

The main fact governing English life since 1939—a fact so obvious that it is frequently overlooked altogether—is the loss of power. Great Britain entered the second world war of its own free will—morally compelled by Hitler, it is true, but nevertheless as an independent foreign-policy decision—and took with it overseas possessions which were then at the most extensive they have ever been. Six years later it emerged from an exhausting struggle as the weakest member of a world triumvirate. . . . With empty currency reserves, an empire demanding self-government, and the world contested between two powers whose home territory was continental in scale and whose populations were numbered in hundreds, instead of tens of millions, it was obvious that Britain's activities in the world would in future be dwarfed, and that, though statesmen might flatter themselves with a permanent seat on the Security Council of the United Nations and a place at any meeting of the "Big Three" or "Four", the brutal reality was that some countries were very much "bigger" than others.

No major party in Britain proposes that the country should withdraw from world affairs, or believes that she is regarded by other countries as too exhausted to speak or act in international affairs. The Conservative Party insists on the maintenance of Britain's independent nuclear deterrent as a symbol of the country's continuing international power. The Labour and Liberal parties, though ready to abandon Britain's independent deterrent as an expensive and dangerous irrelevance, both claim that Britain still has a valuable rôle to play in world affairs partly through her membership of various alliances and partly because she remains a great trading nation and has long experience of government on a world scale which might assist particularly the newly independent countries.

The difficulty has been to give a new content to the "greatness" of which Britain is now capable, so that the nation may accept a new rôle in the world with honour. Politicians who underrate national pride make a great mistake. The Soviet Union's fight against nazi Germany was stiffened by the evocation of Russia's past history. The message which Sir Winston Churchill sent to President Kennedy on April 6, 1963, accepting honorary citizenship of the United States was a characteristic reassertion of Britain's national pride:

It is a remarkable comment on our affairs that the former Prime Minister of a great sovereign State should thus be received as an honorary citizen of another. I say "great sovereign State" with design and emphasis, for I reject the view that Britain and the Commonwealth should now be relegated to a tame and minor rôle in the world. Our past is the key to our future, which I firmly believe will be no less fertile and glorious. Let no man underrate our energies, our potentialities and our abiding power for good.'

At the same time, politicians cannot afford to ignore the reality of their country's position. To ignore it would be to run the risk of a great catastrophe, and it is not unpatriotic to discover the facts. While the political parties are working out the means by which Britain's future may continue to be "fertile and glorious", the facts of change in Britain's status have become more plain to the country as a whole in the last few years.

Two events in particular have contributed to this result: the outcome of the Anglo-French landings at Suez in 1956, and Britain's application to join the European Economic Community which was made in July 1961, and rejected, at the instance of the French government under President de Gaulle's leadership, early in 1963. The history of the Suez landings showed that Britain and France, acting together, were not strong enough to support a conventional military campaign when financial backing was denied by the United States. Even so, at least half the British nation wished the Suez campaign to succeed.

Mr Hartley makes this comment on British policy in the Middle East:

The granting of independence to India and Pakistan [in 1947] took away both the basis and the *raison d'être* of British suzerainty in that area since the

17

function of this had been to secure the route to India and its maintenance secured by a numerous Indian army a few days' steaming distance from Basra. From Palestine to Egypt to Cyprus, up to 1956 and beyond, successive British Governments continued to behave as though there were still a Viceroy in New Delhi and as if President Nasser were Arabi Pasha. The oilfields of the Middle East provided an easy rationalisation for the traditional idea that we must keep some kind of control over that area, though it is not clear why trade in this particular commodity should have to be protected by military bases any more than that in, say, Argentine beef or Indian tea. The emotions appealed to, however, were the ones which had always been stirred by the idea of a threat to the Indian life-line, and even oil, with its strategic overtones (the fleet, the air force) was calculated to call into action reflexes conditioned by an earlier age.[3]

The attempt to secure Britain's entry into the European Economic Community showed the British public that the Macmillan government foresaw a lessening of Britain's economic and political power in world affairs unless the country became a member of a regional grouping with a consequential loss of a degree of sovereignty and thus of political independence. The government accepted the fact that Britain was too small a market to absorb the increasing exports of other Commonwealth countries, as Harold Macmillan[4] told his colleagues at the Commonwealth Prime Ministers' Conference in London in the summer of 1962.

Later that year (October 13, 1962), Macmillan described Britain's position in a speech to the Conservative Party at Llandudno. He said that in point of numbers Britain was and always had been a relatively weak country, and had therefore always used the instrument of coalition, of alliances, in war.

> In peace perhaps we have used it less. But anyone who looks honestly at the history of the first half of this century cannot help feeling that the prospects of peace might have been better if we had played in peacetime as large a part in the affairs of Europe as we, and our Commonwealth partners, too, have in war. For this hesitation we have paid a heavy price.[5]

To go into Europe, he said, must involve some pooling of national freedom of action, but Britain would become part of, and have free access to, a "home" market of 250 million people instead of 50 million. "It will make possible specialisation and mass production of techniques like automation which can be developed only on the basis of a large home market. The whole trend of modern industry is towards a larger, unified market." At the same time, he stated that Britain's value to the Commonwealth depended not just on sentiment or goodwill, important as they were, but on the economic strength of Britain.

> The Commonwealth (said Macmillan) is not and does not expect to be an economic unity. Nor is it any longer the close-knit military and political alliance between countries of similar origins and all owing allegiance to the Crown which we knew so well during two world wars. The Commonwealth to-day is remarkable for its diversity which is widespread. Indeed, its diversity is its greatest strength. This unique and free association, embracing every creed and race, stretched over five continents and comprising a quarter of the globe's population, is at once an influence and an example of the possibilities of co-operation throughout the world. Its value to peace is incalculable, but I am persuaded that it is

complementary and not alternative to the consolidation of Europe.[6]

This passage illustrates the attempt of a Prime
Minister and party leader to guide his supporters gently
into new courses. The fact that Britain's application to
join the European Economic Community failed was
certainly not Macmillan's fault. The justification he made
for the attempt to enter was accepted by the Liberal
Party, which had been the first party in Britain to advocate entry, but not by Labour, most of whose members
doubted whether any terms likely to be agreed would be
in Britain's true interest. The argument over this issue
was part of the process of forcing the British people to
look at the nature of the changing world.

The events which, since 1945, have pointed to
change may be grouped into three categories—economic,
diplomatic and social—which overlap or interact at
various points. It has become quite apparent that the
balance of trade upon which British governments count
as a test of the country's economic strength is extremely
fine. A period of economic expansion at home may at
once lead to soaring exports and an adverse balance. A
period of restraint, to put the matter right, may quite
soon threaten full employment. Clearly, therefore, the
efficient operation of the British economy demands careful adjustments with the assent of all concerned, particularly the workers and employers. But assent of this kind
implies modifications of older practices by trade unions
and employers' associations, which take time and persua-
sion to bring about.

It has also become apparent that the growth of
exports to Britain from other Commonwealth countries,
which is essential if those countries are to maintain, and
still more to improve, the living standards of their grow-

ing populations, may make Britain's system of free entry for Commonwealth goods unwelcome to particular industries in Britain. The Lancashire cotton textile industry, for example, is united in its opposition to the uncontrolled entry of cotton textiles from Hong Kong, India and Pakistan. A scheme of voluntary restriction has been applied, but no one can doubt that each of these three areas must increase its exports—somehow—if it is to flourish.

The growing economic power of Western Europe and of Russia challenge Britain to make her goods more competitive in world markets and to stimulate world demand by capital investment or by loans or gifts overseas; but Britain's ability to export capital depends itself on the state of Britain's balance of payments. Some of Britain's basic industries are declining: cotton, coal and some branches of engineering, for example ship and locomotive building. New industries—electronics and nuclear power—have been developed since 1945, but the rate at which new industry can replace the old depends partly on the volume and quality of research, technological skill and craftsmanship which are available. Here Britain suffers from her inability to match the resources of the United States and the Soviet Union. The Soviet advance has been remarkable; and there has been, in the field of science, a "brain drain" from Britain to the United States.

Another marked change has occurred in the trend of world trade. Britain entered a period of protection in 1931, when a Conservative-dominated National coalition government was formed. This period persisted until the early years following the second world war. The influences of the United Nations, which came into existence on October 24, 1945, and of the United States, whose interests are bound to affect the course of world trade, combined to promote anti-protectionist policies. Britain subscribed to the General Agreement on Tariffs and Trade which came into force on January 1, 1948. Later in that year Britain became a member of the Organisation for European Economic Co-operation (now the Organisation for Economic Co-operation and Development) which was formed to co-ordinate the economic activities of countries receiving aid under the United States European Recovery Programme—"Marshall Aid", so named after General George Marshall who was then Secretary of State in the United States. On November 20, 1959, Britain became a member of the European Free Trade Association which set out to remove all import duties and quantitative restrictions from trade between members of the Association by January 1, 1970. This Association was formed by seven Western European countries as a means of self-protection after six others had established the European Economic Community under the Treaty of Rome, signed on March 25, 1957.

These changes have had the effect of limiting the efforts of those in Britain who would prefer to expand Commonwealth trade first and international trade second.

Britain's diplomatic position—using the term to cover all her overseas relations—has been studied by the public in several major events. In February 1959, Harold Macmillan went to Moscow in search of better relations between East and West. Public opinion in Britain would have welcomed a happy outcome, but in fact, although Macmillan claimed afterwards to have broken the ice between Moscow and Washington, no very obvious benefits followed. The Summit meeting held in Paris in May 1960 was abortive. It seemed that no agreement was possible, however zealously Britain might promote it, unless the United States and the Soviet Union themselves were willing to agree.

In May 1961 the Union of South Africa withdrew from the Commonwealth and became a Republic. The Union government acted thus because of the opposition of other Commonwealth governments to the South African policy of racial segregation—apartheid. Before South Africa's withdrawal, the issue was considered by the Commonwealth prime ministers in London, but it was obviously impossible for the leaders of black or coloured nations in the Commonwealth to conceal their detestation of apartheid. Leaders of some of the older countries in the Commonwealth were reluctant to force South Africa into withdrawal but could find no means of avoiding this result. The event gave special point to Macmillan's reference in his Llandudno speech to the changing nature of the Commonwealth.

The most stark revelation of Britain's new position, however, occurred in 1962 when the United States administration insisted on the dismantling of nuclear bases in Cuba which the Russians were equipping as a threat to the United States. President Kennedy acted quickly and alone—and his action certainly involved a risk of nuclear war. The mere statement of the facts is enough to show why the British public, after Cuba, questioned the nature of the "special relation" which was supposed to exist between the United States and her closest ally, Britain. How far was Britain to be allowed to share in decisions which might lead the Western Alliance into nuclear war?

Change has been no less evident in the life of the community in Britain. During the Labour governments of 1945-51 the social services were greatly expanded (not invented, as Labour seems sometimes to claim) and the national health service was introduced as an elaboration of an older and narrower state medical system. Basic industries were nationalised and "full employment" was declared to be the principal object of economic policy at

23

home. These changes were expected by the more idealistic Labour supporters to lead to the establishment of virtually a new society in which the bulk of the nation would at last find an outlet for energies of body and mind which had hitherto been cramped by the rigours and inequalities of the capitalist system.

Some of this dream was realised but, for a variety of reasons, by no means all. As a result, some social frustrations were left when Labour was driven out of office. Conservative governments since 1951 retained full employment as their economic objective and kept the main structure of the social services. They altered the pattern a little. They ended food subsidies, for example, but increased the rate of house building with a new emphasis on private as opposed to municipal building. Conservative governments had more room for manoeuvre than the Labour governments had found. As the war receded, and the shortages which followed its end became less, successive governments were able to spend more of the growing national income on housing, hospitals, roads, and similar services.

The Conservatives hoped to secure a sufficiently prosperous social base to permit a gradual redistribution of the national wealth back from the mass of the community, who had been the principal beneficiaries of Labour's rule, towards individuals of enterprise who, in the Conservative view, would use their greater resources to create more wealth. But this policy, too, has led to some frustrations. A rise in the general level of prosperity stimulates demand for goods and this in turn tends to produce an adverse balance of payments through larger imports. Moreover, the contrast between the incomes of the wealthy and those of the average wage-earner is seen to be so great, through what is learned from magazine articles, films, television, advertising and press reports, that a further stimulus is given to the demand of the masses for a still higher standard of life.

When a period of boom is followed by a bout of austerity, the government warns the public that there must be some system of control in the country's economic life. This is particularly the case if Britain is to accumulate capital for use overseas: a service which all the major political parties in Britain value as one sign that their country still has an international rôle to play.

One of the main lessons learned from Britain's economic vicissitudes since 1945 is, therefore, that it is risky to allow economic forces in Britain too much freedom. The Macmillan government in the last year or two began to take rather hesitant steps towards more stringent economic planning from the centre and towards a national incomes policy. But it has acted without the full co-operation of the trade unions, representing the majority of wage earners. Thus, the Conservative Party, which attacked the Labour governments of 1945-51 for planning too much, has itself been driven to accept the need for considerable central planning. The Liberals propose a middle course: more central planning than the Conservatives would choose, but less than Labour believes to be essential.

II

LABOUR GAINS POWER

THE general election of 1945 ended a period in which the Conservatives had dominated successive coalition governments for fourteen years and put the Labour Party in power for the first time in its history. There had been two previous Labour governments (1923-24 and 1929-31) but both were at the mercy of Conservative and Liberal members whenever they chose to act together. These anti-Labour majorities in the House of Commons effectively prevented the first two Labour governments from attempting to introduce extreme socialist measures, even if the Labour Prime Minister, Ramsay MacDonald, and his cabinet colleagues had wished to do so.

The history of Labour in office between the two world wars had, therefore, left a sense of irritation among the more ardent socialists, and when Labour gained power in 1945 some of them doubted whether the new government would introduce the kind of socialist legislation which they wanted. Labour's political opponents, relying on the experiences of the two Labour minority governments, naturally suggested that Labour was unfit to run the country. In fact, the government formed by Clement Attlee (later Lord Attlee) in 1945 governed firmly and introduced socialist measures.

Labour's increase in strength is shown in these tables

which are based on the results of the general elections from 1929 to 1945:

TABLE I
Membership of the House of Commons

Party	1929	1931	1935	1945
Labour	288	52	154	393
Conservative				
and allies	260	521	432	213
Liberals	59	37	20	12
Others	8	5	9	22
Total membership	615	615	615	640

TABLE II
Votes cast (millions)

Party	1929	1931	1935	1945
Labour	8·4	6·6	8·3	12·0
Conservative				
and allies	8·6	13·1	11·8	10·0
Liberals	5·3	1·5	1·4	2·2
Others	0·3	0·4	0·5	0·8
Total	22·6	21·6	22·0	25·0

It will be seen from these tables that Labour had an ample majority of members over those of all other parties combined in the House of Commons in 1945, although in terms of votes cast the electorate was about equally divided for and against socialism as represented by the Labour Party's policy. This result of the electoral system must be considered later. Britain accepted the fact in 1945 that Labour had won an overwhelming victory. Why did it happen? Broadly because there was a strong current of feeling in Britain against a return to pre-war Conservatism which was identified by millions of voters with mass unemployment, which had devastated the community between the wars; with resistance to any system of collective security such as had been hoped for from the old League of Nations; with tolerance of the nazi and fascist dictatorships; and with a traditional economic pattern thought to be incapable of making the changes which large sections of the public demanded in 1945.

In retrospect, much of this criticism of pre-war Conservatism seems to have been insecurely based, but there was no mistaking the public's mood in favour of change. In particular, there was a positive horror of a return to the conditions of mass unemployment. The first world war had been followed by a long period of industrial turmoil: strikes by the trade unionists, and lockouts by the employers. Nobody wanted that to recur after the second world war. Moreover, Labour still remembered the consequences of Britain's return to the gold standard in 1925 when Churchill had been Chancellor of the Exchequer in a Conservative government. Britain abandoned the gold standard in the first world war, but orthodox economists persuaded Churchill that Britain's position in the world would be strengthened if she restored the standard. In fact, the return to the gold standard in 1925 worsened Britain's economy and led to the General Strike of 1926.

It was not only Conservatives who favoured a return to the gold standard. Philip Snowden, who was Chancellor of the Exchequer in the Labour government of 1929, favoured it, too; and it was only abandoned in the economic crisis of 1931. But, while it is true that politicians of different parties in the 1930s supported orthodox financial methods, the public in 1945 had been taught by John Maynard Keynes (later Lord Keynes), the economist, and by Hugh Dalton, who became Chancellor of the Exchequer in 1945, and by others, that a managed economy was better suited to the ups and downs of world trade.

Social lessons, as well as economic lessons, had been learnt since pre-war days. The second world war had led the British to live as a community more intensively than they had ever done. More people than ever before were directly concerned with the conduct of the struggle. This was the first war which Britain had entered with general conscription in force. All the men, except for those in essential industries and services, were liable to be called up into the armed forces from the start. Supply of the forces made great demands on exempted labour. And the nazis brought the battle into Britain, with a threat of actual invasion which had not been paralleled since the days of Napoleon. The British had to prepare to defend their homeland. They had to ask themselves how they would behave if Britain were occupied by the nazis. They suffered a long series of heavy air raids, first by manned bombers and later by automatic missiles. The evacuation of mothers and children from the more exposed parts of the country became essential, and the results of evacuation taught the British more about themselves, more quickly and directly, than a decade of speeches would have done. Quiet, orderly lives in the areas which received the evacuees were often disrupted by the impact of children from the cities who brought with them the habits they had picked up in grossly overcrowded houses. The children from the cities, and some of their parents, were equally dismayed by the stillness of country life and by the reserve with which life may be lived outside urban clamour. The evacuees and their hosts alike suffered a social shock, to which, in most cases, they adapted themselves.

A more general effect of war-time conditions in Britain was the discovery that people of widely differing social backgrounds could live and work together with mutual respect, and even enjoyment, when they had to share common tasks, common danger and common shortages of food and materials. At no period in modern times, and certainly not during the first world war, were the British more united than they were from 1939 to 1945. A minority of the public, for various reasons, disapproved of Britain's entry into the war; but the great majority, however fearful of the consequences, agreed that Britain was compelled to challenge the nazis in 1939. This broad approval of national policy carried with it general acceptance of the restrictions of war-time living. The effect of this, in political terms, was to show to millions of voters that central planning and control, which Labour advocated, need not lead to the misery and frustration of individuals—provided that the bulk of the country shared a common purpose.

Was there a common purpose in Britain after the military victory of 1945? Conservatives wished to end restrictions on individual enterprises as quickly as possible. That, in their view, would be the best way to make Britain economically prosperous again. But Labour's purpose was different. It was to re-establish the economy on a more equitable basis than had existed before, and to use whatever controls were necessary for the task: to apply a system of priorities so that supplies which were short after the war should be used where they were most needed. This difference of approach to post-war reconstruction developed as the war receded so that to a part of the community the restrictions of war-time began to appear more irksome than in fact they had been when they were being experienced.

Many people in Britain and overseas assumed in 1945 that the British electors would choose Churchill to lead them into peace. His reputation, as the leader of the war-time Coalition government, was at its peak. He had gained Britain the victory. His intellectual and physical powers had not begun to fail. But the majority of the electors in 1945 rejected him not because he was at the head of a party, but because his party was Conservative.

The Conservatives of 1945 were regarded by many electors as the direct heirs of the Conservatives of 1931, although by the end of the war the Conservative Party, whose ability to change with the times explains its persistence in British politics, had already adopted policies that were different from those of pre-war days. Churchill's position as leader of the Conservatives was in any case a little ambiguous. He had never been a sound party man and indeed had been kept out of office by the Conservative Party controllers from 1931, when the National government was formed, until the outbreak of war in 1939. Only the compulsions of war, and a widespread recognition among politicians that his gifts should be brought to the service of the country, persuaded the bulk of the Conservative Party in Parliament to accept Churchill's entry into Neville Chamberlain's government.

This suspicion of Churchill, incredible though it may have seemed to friends of Britain overseas, was the quite intelligible result of the party system. He had first been elected to the House of Commons as a Conservative. He then became a Liberal, and, as a member of Liberal governments from 1906 to 1915, was one of the most ferocious assailants of those Conservatives—the core of their party—who advocated protectionism and opposed Home Rule for Ireland. Later, he became a Conservative again—and stayed one.

Churchill has himself explained the delicacy of his relations with the Conservative Party when he became Prime Minister in May 1940, in succession to Neville Chamberlain who remained, for the time being, leader of the Conservative Party. In his book, *Their Finest Hour*,[1] Churchill writes of the formation of his Coalition government when places had to be found for Labour and Liberal ministers in substitution for Conservatives:

> The Conservatives had a majority of more than one hundred and twenty over all other parties in the House combined. Mr Chamberlain was their chosen leader. I could not but realise that this supression must be very unpleasant to many of them, after all my long years of criticism and fierce reproach. Besides this, it must be evident to the majority of them how my life had been passed in friction or in actual strife with the Conservative Party, that I had left them on Free Trade and had later returned to them as Chancellor of the Exchequer. After that I had been for many years their leading opponent on India, on foreign policy, and on the lack of preparations for war. To accept me as Prime Minister was to them very difficult. It caused pain to many honourable men. Moreover, loyalty to the chosen leader of the party is a prime characteristic of the Conservatives. If they had on some questions fallen short of their duty to the nation in the years before the war, it was because of this sense of loyalty to their appointed chief. None of these considerations caused me the slightest anxiety. I knew they were all drowned by the cannonade.

In October 1940, Chamberlain resigned the leadership of the Conservative Party because he was mortally ill. Churchill was invited to take his place, and he has explained why he did so:

> I had to ask myself the question—about which there may still be various opinions—whether the leadership of one great party was compatible with the position I held from the King and Parliament as Prime Minister of an administration composed of

and officially supported by, all parties. I had no doubt about the answer. The Conservative Party possessed a very large majority in the House of Commons over all other parties combined. Owing to the war conditions no election appeal to the nation was available in case of disagreement or deadlock. I should have found it impossible to conduct the war if I had had to procure the agreement in the compulsive days of crisis and during the long years of adverse and baffling struggle not only of the leaders of the two minority parties but of the leader of the Conservative majority. Whoever had been chosen and whatever his self-denying virtues he would have had the real power. For me there would have been only the executive responsibility.

These arguments do not apply in the same degree in time of peace; but I do not feel I could have borne such a trial successfully in war. Moreover, in dealing with the Labour and Liberal parties in the Coalition it was always an important basic fact that as Prime Minister and at this time Leader of the largest party I did not depend upon their votes and I could in the ultimate issue carry on in Parliament without them. I therefore accepted the position of Leader of the Conservative Party which was pressed upon me, and I am sure that without it, and all the steady loyalties which attached to it, I should not have been able to discharge my task until victory was won.[2]

Churchill had himself seen, when he had been a member of Lloyd George's Coalition governments during and after the first world war, the weakness of the position of a Prime Minister who was not also the leader of a majority party in the House of Commons. The shifts to which Lloyd George was put as Prime Minister have been catalogued by Lord Beaverbrook in his books, *Men and Power*[3] and *The Decline and Fall of Lloyd George*.[4] Even after Churchill had become leader of the Conservatives, as well as Prime Minister, his relations with his party remained uneasy.

An assessment of the Conservative attitude to Sir Winston was made in March 1945 by Harry Boardman who, as a journalist, had described the proceedings of Parliament throughout the second world war. In his book, *The Glory of Parliament*, he wrote:

> At bottom the Tories during the war have not taken Mr Churchill to their bosoms much more than they did in the inter-war years. . . . Their reservations about Mr Churchill have not always been concealed. When he became Prime Minister in 1940 there was no rejoicing on the Tory benches. Indeed, there was something much more like silence. It was left to Labour to applaud Mr Churchill when he entered the House. Not for some time did this Tory reserve break down. But even the Tories could not for ever withhold admiration from the country's saviour.[5]

This summary of party considerations helps to explain why Churchill's prestige alone was not enough in 1945 to convince many electors that the party he led had changed its spots. In any case, suspicions of him were felt by some members of other parties. While many Liberals still liked to think of him as a member of the 1906 Liberal government, others had been shocked by his resistance to constitutional reform in India between the two world wars. Hosts of Labour Party supporters regarded him as the most formidable opponent in Britain of socialism and of the organised workers. Two events in his career led Labour's rank and file to distrust him as a peace-time minister: a distrust which persisted for forty

years or so. The facts in each case have been disputed,
but there can be no question of the hostile emotional
reaction set up among many Labour supporters on both
occasions.

In 1910, when Churchill was Home Secretary in a
Liberal government and was responsible for the maintenance of law and order in Britain, he authorised the despatch of troops to South Wales in support of the police
during a period of grave industrial unrest in the coal
fields. At Tonypandy, miners tried to attack a colliery
from which the owners had locked them out, but they
were driven off by the local police. Troops were not
present at the time: they arrived later. "Tonypandy" became, however, a call to battle in Labour's subsequent
political attacks on Churchill. The cry was still heard in
South Wales during the general election of 1950, and
Churchill himself, speaking in Cardiff during that campaign, said it was a "cruel lie" to charge him with having
sent troops to attack the miners. Though he had authorised the despatch of troops, he had taken special care to
reinforce the police, the normal protectors of the peace
in civil life, and to limit the number of troops which were
sent to South Wales.

The second event occurred when he was Chancellor
of the Exchequer in 1926 in Stanley Baldwin's government. Churchill was one of the most active ministers in
organising emergency measures to control and defeat the
General Strike which took place in May of that year with
the support of the Trades Union Congress, the central
authority of the trade union movement. His zest for
action in periods of national emergency, which served
Britain so well in the second world war, marked him for
trade unionists as their special enemy. The construc-
tive work which he had done in the 1906 government in
helping to lay the foundations of the social security
system which has now turned Britain into a "Welfare

State" was not remembered in his favour in 1926 by the more militant socialists.

At the start of the 1945 election campaign, therefore, factors were at work which diverted support both from Churchill himself, because of his record as a peacetime minister, and from the Conservative Party. In the course of the campaign he alienated more support by his own tactics. He made two charges against the Labour Party which were deeply resented not only by Labour supporters but by people of more moderate opinion.

In his first election broadcast (June 4, 1945), he said that the logical development of the socialist policy of the Labour Party was incompatible with Britain's democratic system, was abhorrent to the British idea of freedom, and inseparably interwoven with totalitarianism and the abject worship of the state. No socialist system, he said, could be established without a political police. "They would have to fall back upon some form of Gestapo, no doubt very humanely directed in the first instance," he declared. This "Gestapo" broadcast is estimated to have cost the Conservatives hundreds of thousands of votes. Churchill was speaking of Labour leaders—Clement Attlee, Ernest Bevin, Herbert Morrison, Hugh Dalton—well known to the British public and with whom he himself had been working, until a few weeks earlier, in harmony and loyalty. These men had all been with him in the Coalition government which had one over-riding purpose: to beat nazi Germany with its Gestapo and its gas chambers. No doubt Churchill's real target was the political police of Soviet Russia, but in 1945 Russia was Britain's ally. To identify the social democracy of the British Labour Party with a Gestapo system, at such a moment, struck many electors as an act of crass stupidity at best and, at worst, an act of wicked malice.

His second charge against Labour was made in the fourth and last of his election broadcasts (June 30, 1945). He said in effect that a Labour government would be primarily responsible not to the Crown and to Parliament—the traditional constitutional line of responsibility—but to the Labour Party's national executive committee, which, he claimed, had far-reaching powers over socialist ministers.

The origin of this charge must be explained in some detail because it illustrates a perpetual cause of controversy in the Labour movement: how directly should Labour ministers (as members of a democratic party, as Churchill might have remembered) be made subject to the decisions of the rank and file through the established organs of the party: the annual delegate conference and the national executive committee? No government in Britain can survive if it forfeits the support of the party or parties on which it rests, but the constitutional practice is for a government to be autonomous to this extent: that it makes its own decisions, having assessed the state of public and party opinion. It does not wait to act until a party conference or a party executive has first decided what it should do. The British government is in theory the government of the country and not a mere group of party leaders, just as a member of the House of Commons represents all his constituents and not simply those who voted for him.

The charge that a Labour government would be subordinate to the party's national executive committee was made as the result of the action of the then chairman of the Labour Party, Professor Harold Laski, a distinguished teacher of politics and economics. He was once described in an official Labour Party publication as "the foremost British authority on the history of Communism". Although Laski's reputation as a teacher and as an exponent of the theory of socialism remained

37

throughout his life extremely high, both in Britain and in the United States, he was never regarded by the general public as an important figure in British political life. Election to the chairmanship of the Labour Party is no guarantee of political wisdom or distinction. It is an honour awarded to members of the national executive committee on the basis of seniority of service.

As chairman of the Labour Party, Laski tried to control the freedom of action of Attlee, who was then leader, as well as leader of the opposition in the House of Commons. (Churchill's Coalition government, in which Attlee had been Deputy Prime Minister, ended in May 1945, when Labour and the Liberals went into opposition.) Professor Laski's experiment in control was made when Churchill, as Prime Minister of the "Caretaker" government, invited Attlee, as leader of the opposition, to accompany him to the Potsdam Conference between the leaders of the United States, the Soviet Union and Britain. This invitation was sent because the result of the general election of 1945 would not be known when the Potsdam Conference met, and it was thought prudent that Attlee and Churchill, either of whom might find himself Prime Minister as a result of the election, should both take part in the proceedings and decisions of the Conference. This was the timetable: Parliament was dissolved on June 15, 1945. Polling took place on July 5, but the result was not declared until July 26 to allow time for the collection of votes from members of the armed forces serving overseas. The Potsdam Conference opened on July 17—after the poll had closed but before the result was known.

Attlee accepted Churchill's invitation to go to Potsdam, and Professor Laski then made a statement. The effect of it was this: the Potsdam Conference would discuss matters which neither Labour's national executive committee nor the Parliamentary Labour Party had considered. Labour, therefore, could not be committed to the decisions of the Conference, and Attlee, if he went to Potsdam, must go only as an observer and must not accept responsibility for agreements made by Churchill as head of a Conservative government. This was Laski's view as Labour's chairman.

Churchill wrote to Attlee on June 15 stating that while the government must accept responsibility for all the decisions made at Potsdam, it would be derogatory to Attlee's position as leader of the Labour Party if he went as a mute observer. The Labour leader replied that he had accepted the invitation to go to Potsdam in agreement with his principal colleagues in the House of Commons, and added that there had never been any suggestion that he should go as a mute observer. He saw great public advantage "in preserving and presenting to the world at this time that unity on foreign policy which we maintained throughout the last five years".

When Churchill returned to the "Laski" theme in his broadcast of June 30, Attlee replied that "the insinuation that Labour ministers have so little respect for their oaths as Privy Councillors that they will reveal cabinet and military secrets to outsiders"—for example, to members of Labour's national executive committee who might be neither Privy Councillors nor members of Parliament—"is vile and false".

Churchill had not done with Professor Laski yet. He wrote to Attlee on July 2 agreeing that he was not aware of any case in which Labour's national executive committee had demanded secret information from Labour ministers who had served in the Coalition government, but commented that powers, hitherto latent, had been asserted in a surprising manner by Laski as chairman of the Labour Party. He noted that Professor Laski had not withdrawn his original Potsdam statement, and had been disavowed neither by Labour's national executive committee nor by the Labour Party.

Attlee replied again. Only a few days were now left before the electors went to the poll and Labour had no intention of giving the Conservatives a chance to frighten the voters with a "Red" scare, as had happened once before, in the general election of 1924. He gave Churchill an account of the constitutional relation of the Labour Party's national executive committee with the Parliamentary Labour Party which, he said, had existed for years. "Neither by decision of the annual party conference, nor by any provision in the party constitution", he wrote, "is the Parliamentary Labour Party answerable to or under the direction of the national executive committee. Within the programme adopted by the annual party conference, the Parliamentary Labour Party has complete discretion in its conduct of parliamentary business and in the attitude it should adopt to legislation tabled by other parties." Naturally, he wrote, there were consultations between the Parliamentary Party and the national executive committee, but "at no time and in no circumstances has the national executive committee ever sought to give, or given, instructions to the Parliamentary Labour Party arising out of the consultations. . . . The chairman has not power to give me instructions."

On July 3, only two days before the poll, Churchill renewed his attack on the Laski position. In fact, he had left so little time before the poll opened that he was suspected of having attempted to deprive Attlee of the right of reply. This was noted with indignation by Labour's supporters. But Attlee did reply. Churchill's final demand was that Attlee and Laski should jointly sign a statement on the future use of the powers of Labour's national executive committee. The Labour leader retorted: "Despite my very clear statement, you proceed to exercise your imagination by importing into a right to be consulted a power to challenge actions and conduct." In demanding a joint statement, wrote Attlee, Churchill was underestimating the intelligence of the public. In the end, Attlee went to Potsdam on his own terms and won the election.

So much for the failure of the Conservatives in 1945. Labour's success was secured partly by the negative action of voters in keeping the Conservatives out, but mainly by a positive movement of opinion in favour of radical changes in British society. Labour had fought the 1945 general election on a programme, *Let Us Face the Future*, which was the result of many months of preparation. The programme advocated the maintenance of full employment; the public ownership of coal, gas and electricity; of inland transport; and of the iron and steel industries; and all on the basis of fair compensation for the private owners. Labour described its ultimate goal as the establishment of a Socialist Commonwealth, but added that socialism could not come overnight and that the programme must be selective: sufficient for one parliament, which would normally last just under five years. Labour also proposed to bring the Bank of England under public ownership, to supervise monopolies and cartels, and to maintain economic and price controls on essential supplies in order to protect priorities in the period of transition after the war. *Let Us Face the Future* stated plainly that the Labour Party did not wish to retain or impose controls for the sake of control, but as a safeguard "against the chaos which would follow the end of all public control". The programme promised a comprehensive social security system and a national health service, and public authorities were to have greater power to acquire land.

The fear of post-war chaos, which sprang from remembrance of Britain's discomforts after the first world war, was a powerful element in the electors' minds and was so recognised by the three parties—Conservative,

Labour and Liberal—which had been represented in the war-time Coalition government. That government had itself taken steps, well before the war was over, to prepare plans to guard against social disruption when the fighting stopped. In fact, all three parties recognised in their election manifestoes in 1945 that some of the war-time controls were bound to be continued for a time during the period of transition to a peace economy. (What nobody then knew was the length of time it would take to restore a peace-time economy that could be considered normal. What was to be "normal" in the post-war world?)

The difference between the parties lay in the emphasis which each placed on the importance of ending controls as quickly as possible. Churchill's *Declaration of Policy to the Electors* pledged the Conservatives to remove controls as quickly as the need for them disappeared. The Conservatives would "guard the people of this country against those who, under the guise of war necessity, would like to impose upon Britain for their own purposes a permanent system of bureaucratic control, reeking of totalitarianism".

The Liberals' *Radical Programme of Practical Reform* promised that no control should remain longer than was absolutely necessary for the welfare of the country and the full employment of its people.

At the time of the 1945 election, however, many electors were more interested to see social changes made rapidly, with or without controls, than to ask when the controls would end. Here, the Labour Party represented the prevailing popular mood more accurately than did either of its major opponents. Thus, although the Conservatives incorporated in their election programme proposals for the development of the social services and for the maintenance of full employment, which had indeed been outlined by the Coalition government before the end of the war, Labour was thought to be more determined on change. The Conservatives would not allow drastic changes of ownership to be forced on industries "on no evidence except a political theory and with no practical regard to the results they may bring". The Liberals, too, supported full employment and the extension of social security, and favoured the public ownership of the railways and their ancillary services, of electricity and coal (but not of iron and steel). The Liberals proposed that the state should acquire the development rights of land, outside built-up areas, and should impose a levy on all increases in site values. This was certainly a radical programme, but the Liberals were still in a period of decline from their days of power and were not regarded by the electorate as capable of forming an alternative government to that of the Conservatives.

The mood of the public had made itself felt long before the war was over. On December 1, 1942, proposals for the post-war development of the social services were published in a document known as the Beveridge Report. Its origin, its reception by the public, and its treatment by the parties explain a good deal in recent British political history. The war-time Coalition government, despite the almost overwhelming demands of the battle, gave thought to the future of Britain after victory which was assumed to be inevitable in the long run. In May 1941, the government announced that the Minister without Portfolio, Arthur Greenwood, would make a comprehensive survey of social insurance. Greenwood was one of the Labour ministers. He had been Minister of Health in the Labour government of 1929-31 and was one of the most popular and trusted figures in the Labour movement.

Greenwood appointed Sir William Beveridge (later Lord Beveridge), a man of wide experience both of the academic world and of the civil service, to preside over a committee that would prepare a report on social insurance. On completing his task, Sir William explained the broad purpose of his scheme in a broadcast:

> The Atlantic Charter, among other aims, speaks of securing for all "improved labour standards, economic advancement and social security". The security plan in my report is a plan for turning the last two words, "social security", from words into deeds, for securing that no one in Britain willing to work, while he can, is without income sufficient to meet at all times the essential needs of himself and his family.[6]

From the moment of its publication, the Beveridge Report—or, rather, acceptance of the need for a comprehensive extension of social security—became a political test for many people, including particularly those who were serving in the armed forces. Who was for Beveridge and who against? The government gave the impression, at the very moment when public opinion was most excited by the publication of the plan, that it viewed the Beveridge proposals with coldness. This impression had not been removed when the general election of 1945 took place.

The government's position was not easy. Ministers realised far better than the public that Britain's resources might be exhausted when the fighting stopped. Churchill was so sharply aware of this danger that on the very day (January 12, 1943) when he was to leave England for the Casablanca Conference with President Roosevelt, he circulated a note to the cabinet about post-war conditions:

> A dangerous optimism is growing up about the conditions it will be possible to establish here after the war. Unemployment and low wages are to be abolished; education greatly improved and pro-

longed; great developments in housing and health will be undertaken; agriculture is to be maintained at least at its new high level. At the same time, the cost of living is not to be raised. The Beveridge plan of social insurance, or something like it, is to abolish want. The money which the wage-earning classes have saved during the war in nest-eggs or accumulated by War Savings Certificates must not lose its value.

Our foreign investments have almost disappeared. The United States will be a strong competitor with British shipping. We shall have great difficulties in placing our necessary exports profitably. Meanwhile, in order to help Europe, we are to subject ourselves to a prolonged period of rationing and distribute a large part of our existing stocks. We are to develop the tropical Colonies and raise the condition of their inhabitants. We must clearly keep a large Air Force and Navy, so as not to be set upon again by the Germans, and large military forces will be needed to garrison the enemy countries and make sure they do not begin again to rearm for revenge.

The question steals across the mind whether we are not committing our forty-five million people to tasks beyond their capacity to bear. . . . We must all do our best, and we shall do it much better if we are not hampered by a cloud of pledges and promises which arise out of the hopeful and genial side of man's nature and are not brought into relation with the hard facts of life.[7]

This note, circulated less than two months after the Beveridge Report was published, underestimated the hazards that Britain was to face in 1945: the circumstances in which the United States administration was to end the Lease-Lend system, which came into operation in

1943 and which gave Britain essential financial support during the war, were to confront the new Labour government with a massive obstacle. But the harder the facts of life, the more the electors were determined that essential priorities should be secured, if necessary by stringent controls. Among these essential priorities was an extension of social security.

This was made very plain when the House of Commons debated the Beveridge Report in February 1943. By this time Arthur Greenwood, who had left the government before the report came out, was leading the opposition. (While he had remained in office he had given valuable support to Sir William Beveridge and his committee.) Greenwood said in the February debate: "The people of this country have made up their minds to see the plan in its broad outlines carried into effect, and nothing will shift them." That is what the public wanted to hear. Ministers, on the other hand, were cool or cautious in their references to the plan. They failed, almost without exception—Brendan Bracken (later Lord Bracken), a Conservative, who was Minister of Information at the time, was one exception—to measure the flow of feeling in favour of the Beveridge plan that was running among Liberals and some Conservatives, as well as on the Labour side. (Sir William Beveridge was himself a Liberal, and from 1944-45 sat in the House of Commons as Liberal member for Berwick-on-Tweed. When he was created a peer in 1946 he sat as a Liberal in the House of Lords.)

A small group of Conservatives who called themselves the "Tory Reformers" and were led in the House of Commons by Lord Hinchingbrooke (later Lord Sandwich), spoke in favour of immediate action on the Beveridge Report during the February debate. The government took no heed. It went out of its way to advertise to the army its cautious approach to social advance. The

Coalition government had introduced a scheme during the war to explain to the men and women in the forces what Britain was fighting for, and to stimulate discussion. As part of this scheme, an institution called the Army Bureau of Current Affairs (ABCA) prepared a series of pamphlets which were distributed free throughout the army for use by discussion groups. In December 1942, the ABCA subject was the Beveridge Report, which had just been published. Six months later this "Beveridge" pamphlet was replaced by another on social security which warned its readers of the danger of easy promises.

The effect of this switch on groups of British soldiers throughout the world was to force a choice between the Labour and the Churchillian approaches to social advance. Lord Beveridge, writing of the ABCA affair in 1953, stated:

> I doubt whether, after this affair, Mr Churchill could have avoided defeat, whenever a general election came. The troops from this action got it firmly into their heads that for social reform they must look elsewhere than to him. But Mr Churchill could have avoided the decision at the end of the debate of February 16-18, 1943, which marked the Labour Party as the one hope of a better world after the war.[8]

One other factor contributing to the defeat of the Conservatives in 1945 must be mentioned: the effect of joint campaigning against the Conservatives from 1935 to 1939 by members of various parties acting to promote a United Front. The Conservative-dominated National government which had been elected in 1931, and re-elected, with a smaller majority, in 1935, appeared to a section of the public to be set on conciliating—"appeasing" was the word used in the party battle—the dictators of Germany and Italy, Hitler and Mussolini. In desperation, almost, some Labour and Liberal supporters agreed to work with communists in challenging the policies of the National government and in trying to establish in the public's mind an image of the Conservative leaders as dangerous reactionaries. On the Continent, a Popular Front of communists, socialists and others, which had been proposed by the Communist International in 1935, was being developed.

Both the Labour Party and the Trades Union Congress officially condemned the United Front because the communists supported it. Herbert Morrison (later Lord Morrison of Lambeth), who was then a member of the national executive committee of the Labour Party, had the duty, on behalf of the executive, of advising delegates to the Labour Party conference in 1937 to reject a proposal made by Sir Stafford Cripps that Labour should officially enter an alliance of all left-wing parties. The conference rejected the proposal by an overwhelming majority. Lord Morrison stated his own belief in his *Autobiography* that in such an alliance the Communist Party, though puny, "would be able to corrupt the huge Labour Party once it gained a foothold, just as it had done in Europe".[9] Nevertheless, the United Front campaign made an impression in countless meetings throughout Britain, and certainly contributed to the mood which prevented the return of the Conservatives to power in 1945. Two communists were in fact elected to the House of Commons in 1945. One, Willie Gallacher, retained a seat he had held since 1935, but the other, Phil Piratin, was a newcomer. Since 1950 there have been no communists in the House of Commons.

The new parliament met on August 1, 1945. Labour had a majority of nearly two to one in the House of Commons and had been elected to power after the country had been given a clear indication of what a

Labour government would do. There could be no argument about that. In the House of Commons it seemed as though the new government would be able to do just what it wanted. The situation was different in the House of Lords, where the Labour peers were in a minority, but the emphatic verdict of the electors was taken by Labour voters as a clear warning to the Conservative majority in the House of Lords not to be foolish enough to frustrate the Labour government's legislation. This majority had once frustrated the radical programme of a Liberal government with the result that the Parliament Act, 1911, had been passed to curb the power of the House of Lords. In 1945 a majority of the electors—Liberals as well as Labour—were not prepared to allow a hereditary chamber to stop the work of the elected representatives of the people. This situation was to change a little before long.

III

THE PARLIAMENTARY SYSTEM

THE existence of a permanent Conservative majority in the House of Lords created a problem for the new Labour government, but in 1945 this was not considered to be pressing. A more urgent question was whether or not the parliamentary system could take the strain to be imposed on it by the large volume of controversial legislation which the new government was determined to pass through it. This was not simply a matter of the ability of the Conservatives, as the principal opposition party, to obstruct the course of Labour's legislation by all legitimate parliamentary processes, but a question of the efficiency of the parliamentary machine itself. Could the machine work thoroughly enough and fast enough to transform, by constitutional methods, the British economy and society within the span of one parliament —within five years? Some of the members who entered the House of Commons in 1945 for the first time had doubts about its traditional procedures which seemed to them to be archaic, designed to check rapid advance, and part of an old order which had passed away when the minuets danced round No. 10 Downing Street by Whigs and Tories, Liberals and Conservatives, had been shattered by the inrush of Labour members in working clothes.

This was the attitude to Parliament of the more fiery socialists in 1945. They would stand no interruptions of their compulsive law-making by ceremonial delays, such as the arrival of Black Rod at the doors of the House of Commons to summon the members of the House to hear a Royal Commission read in the House of Lords. Black Rod's messages—he is an officer of the House of Lords appointed by letters patent from the sovereign—stop the business of the Commons for half-an-hour or so. What, asked the new Labour members, had such flummery to do with the building of a health service?

It was not only impatient Labour members who doubted the efficiency of the parliamentary system in the modern world. The British people had watched with apprehension the strength of totalitarianism, before and during the second world war, in organising a nation for maximum economic and military effort—in nazi Germany, in fascist Italy, and in Soviet Russia. In Britain itself, before the war, the British Union of Fascists, led by Sir Oswald Mosley, who had formerly been a minister in the Labour government of 1929-31, persistently condemned the parliamentary system as a refuge for the old, the effete, and the creatures of international finance who put interest rates before patriotism. For some months Sir Oswald's fascists had the backing of a national newspaper.

No member of the British Union of Fascists was ever elected to the House of Commons, and no supporter of Sir Oswald's post-war organisation, the Union Movement, which is equally contemptuous of Parliament in its present form, has been elected either. But Sir Oswald had a considerable following in Britain before the war, largely because so many people were scared of unemployment, or were victims of it, and were willing to seek the cause of their wretchedness in the activities of international finance: "the Jews", whom Hitler was busy segregating from German society.

The result of the second world war proved that the totalitarian systems of Hitler and Mussolini, lacking the resources of the Western allies, could not prevail over the United States and Britain with the massive support of the Soviet Union. The governments of the United States and Britain rested on the freely elected assemblies of Congress and Parliament, and to that extent members of Parliament in Britain felt that their system had been gloriously vindicated in the fight against the dictators. But the Soviet government rests on a totalitarian system; and the British Parliament had itself conferred far-reaching powers on the British government for war-time needs.

On August 24, 1939, a few days before Britain entered a war that was then seen to be inevitable, the government was granted virtually complete control over lives and property in the Emergency Powers (Defence) Act. Could the social revolution be made in 1945 without equally drastic powers? Were not strong central controls as essential in peace-time, if a victory was to be won over poverty, as in war-time over a military enemy? Was not the lesson of the war that mass-organisation, implying strong, central management, was indispensable to equip any state for survival in the modern world?

A number of Labour members in the Parliament of 1945 who regarded themselves as guided by the highest national interest thought it probable that Labour's programme could only be applied if Parliament delegated a good deal of its power to the government. This, they felt, would make for swift, effective action. But one block of opinion in the new House of Commons—members of the two parties, Conservative and Liberal, which were in opposition—was not prepared to surrender any of the opposition's constitutional rights to challenge, test, seek to amend, or delay those items in the government's programme to which it objected. Labour's bill to nationalise the gas industry was long resisted during its committee stage by Conservatives led by Brendan Bracken. This demonstration of an opposition at work was more a symbol of the vitality of traditional parliamentary procedure than an attempt to destroy a measure because of its odiousness to the Conservatives. In fact, a national plan for the gas industry had been proposed in 1945 by a committee presided over by Sir Geoffrey Heyworth (later Lord Heyworth), who was no socialist firebrand but the chairman of Unilever Limited, one of Britain's greatest capitalist enterprises.

Not only did the two opposition parties stand upon their constitutional rights, but they claimed that a majority of the electors in 1945 had voted anti-socialist. The figures printed in Table II (p. 27) show that while Labour had won a large majority of the seats in the House of Commons in 1945, the Conservative and Liberal votes combined slightly exceeded the Labour vote. Conservative and Liberal members asserted that Labour had not been authorised by the electors to destroy a constitution which provided checks on the executive. Labour had not sought any such authority in 1945, and indeed powerful figures in the new Labour government were firm constitutionalists: social democrats eager to prove that Labour could govern decisively through the parliamentary processes. The Prime Minister, Clement Attlee, was himself a loyal parliamentarian, and Herbert Morrison, who was Leader of the House of Commons from 1945 to 1951 and was thus directly responsible for the government's attitude to Parliament as an institution, had a taste for ceremonial. He enjoyed the title of his office: Lord President of the Council. As Lord President he was virtually free of departmental duties but had a seat in the cabinet from which he could manage the government's business.

The Labour ministers did not intend to "seize the state" with their elected majority in 1945. The electors by their votes had made remote the temptation to do any such thing.

But the efficiency of the parliamentary system remained an issue in 1945, and still is one. Within recent years doubts have been raised about Parliament's power to check the executive and to make informed judgments on the business of government which becomes ever more far-reaching and complex. These will be examined in more detail later. It is first essential to describe the parliamentary system which is a formal expression of British political life. This is no academic study. The British have been devising systems of government for their dependent territories for a long time. Latterly, many of these territories, on becoming independent, have copied or adapted British practices and have thus posed the question whether they can be transplanted.

The mechanics of the British system are described in the Representation of the People Act, 1949, which since then has been amended only slightly. Great Britain (England, Scotland and Wales) and Northern Ireland are divided into 630 constituencies, each returning one member to the House of Commons at Westminster. Of these constituencies, 511 are in England (289 borough seats and 222 county seats), 71 in Scotland (32 "burgh" seats and 39 county seats), 36 are in Wales (10 borough seats and 26 county seats) and 12 in Northern Ireland (4 borough seats and 8 county seats). Voting is by adult suffrage, and candidates are mostly members of one of the organised parties: Conservative, Labour, Liberal and Communist. Candidates who are independent of any organised party have virtually no chance of election. There are differences of party label among candidates but these are of little significance in terms of policy. The Conservatives, for example, are supported by National Liberals, Scottish Unionists and Ulster Unionists. Labour is supported by "Labour and Co-operative" candidates.

The essence of the system is that each party enters a general election campaign with a statement of policy. The leader of the party which gets the largest number of candidates elected to the House of Commons is invited by the Sovereign to try to form a government, and this he readily attempts. As a rule, the government so formed is maintained in office by the constant support of the majority party in the House of Commons until the time for a new general election arrives, or until the Prime Minister feels that, for a variety of reasons, he can properly ask the Sovereign to dissolve Parliament so that a general election may take place. Under the terms of the Parliament Act, 1911, no Parliament may last longer than five years after the date of its first meeting. In practice, general elections are held on average every four years or so, although special circumstances may vary the interval between elections. The Parliament elected in 1929 was dissolved in 1931 because of a political upheaval caused by a world economic crisis. The Parliament elected in 1935 remained in being until 1945 because of the outbreak of war in 1939: the normal party battle was suspended for the duration of the war. The Parliament elected in 1950 lasted only until 1951 because Labour had too small a majority to support a strong government.

The second largest party in the House of Commons following a general election becomes the official opposition, whose leader is paid a salary by the state. In effect, the official opposition is always ready (or pretends to be) to provide an alternative government to that formed by the majority party. The British parliamentary democracy is thus often described as a "two-party system": one party being in power, and the other anxious to take its place. It is more accurate to write of an "alternative government system" since the party challenging the government might be able to supplant it only with the help of a third party which might, or might not, enter into a coalition to bring this change about. The figures in Table I (p. 27) show that Labour could not have supplanted the Conservatives in 1929 unless the Liberals had approved of the change, but the Liberals did not enter the Labour government and were not invited to do so. When the Conservatives took office in 1951, with a small majority in the House of Commons, a few places were offered to the Liberals, who refused them. In the general election of December 1923, the Conservatives had a larger number of seats in the House of Commons than any other party but were nearly a hundred short of the combined Labour and Liberal total. In these circumstances, the Liberal leader, H. H. Asquith (a former prime minister and later first Earl of Oxford and Asquith), helped Labour to defeat the Conservatives in January 1924, and supported the formation of the first Labour government. In October of the same year, the Liberals helped the Conservatives to defeat Labour, and in the general election which followed the Conservatives returned to power with a majority over all other parties combined. Labour never forgave the Liberals for this action.

The British elector, however, appears to be content with what may roughly be considered as a two-party system: one party being a little to the right, and the other a little to the left, of centre, and each capable of providing an alternative government. The fact that such a system works in Britain implies a degree of homogeneity in British society which may perhaps be indispensable to the effective operation of the system. If the two main parties in the House of Commons are known to the electors to be alternatives in government, and are so accepted, the parliamentary system of government is accepted too. Neither of the two parties contesting for power through Parliament would, it may be assumed, attempt to overthrow the system on securing power. Neither would lightly destroy the safeguards for the opposition since each is liable to find itself in opposition, and in need of those safeguards, from time to time. In theory, any party pledged to autocracy or totalitarianism could, under the parliamentary system, obtain a majority of seats in the House of Commons and at once destroy the system. In practice there has never in modern times been any sign of such a revolution at the polls; and the reason must clearly be that the British system, as it was developed over centuries, produces results which satisfy the majority of the electors.

The creation of a centre party has been discussed by individual members of different parties who have thought that there might be advantage if like-minded men and women from the Conservative, Labour and Liberal parties worked together to promote common interests. When the Labour Party seemed to be fatally divided in 1960-61 on the question of unilateral nuclear disarmament by Britain, moderate opinion suggested that an arrangement between supporters of the centre and right of the Labour Party and of the Liberals might provide the most effective combination to defeat the Conservatives. This group, it was said, shared a common outlook on defence and on Commonwealth affairs and might have agreed on a programme of radical social reform. (By 1963, the possibility of such an arrangement had receded with Labour's recovery of a greater sense of unity.) This proposal for common action was never discussed officially by the Labour and Liberal Parties and would almost certainly have been rejected by the rank and file of both. The creation of a strong centre party, however attractive it may seem, would carry a grave danger with it. The assembly of the moderates of the Conservative, Labour and Liberal Parties into one dominant group in Parliament would stimulate the growth of extreme parties of left and right: the communists and fascists would gain and threaten the stability of political life in Britain.

There are obvious advantages in the alternative government system. It provides a means of making radical changes by consent—in effect a bloodless revolution. It is a delicately controlled release-mechanism for social tension, and the results have general validity because they are secured by means acceptable to both the contending parties. The two principal contending parties since 1924 have been the Conservatives and Labour; and they represent public opinion to this extent that in the general election of 1959 they polled together nearly 26 million votes out of a total of just under 28 million votes.

At times, the issues between the parties are so controversial that the parliamentary system of balances is itself threatened. There have been two occasions when the reluctance of the House of Lords to pass legislation approved by an elected majority in the House of Commons led the government of the time to propose the creation of peers to swamp the opposition in the House of Lords. The first occasion was the Whig government's Reform Bill of 1832, and the second was the Parliament Bill of 1911, introduced by Asquith's Liberal government to prevent the House of Lords from killing financial proposals. In neither case was the threat to make more peers put into operation. At the last moment, the House of Lords yielded to the House of Commons.

Only once in modern times has an organised party in the House of Commons tried systematically to disrupt the parliamentary system. The efforts of the Irish Nationalists to bring the work of the House of Commons to a standstill unless its own grievances were redressed shows how essential political homogeneity is to the working of the British system. The Irish Nationalists were not prepared to consider the claims of British politics until their country had recovered political freedom. The British parliamentary system, when transplanted to a country consisting of deeply divided factions or of different racial groups, may operate imperfectly or develop a different character from that of the system in operation at Westminster.

In 1800, the Irish Parliament in Dublin, imperfect though it was from the nationalists' point of view, was abolished to the detriment of Ireland. An Act of Union with Britain provided for the representation of the Irish in the parliament at Westminster. Irish members were elected to the House of Commons from 1801 to 1918, but the Anglo-Irish Treaty of 1921 established Southern Ireland as a Free State and its link with Westminster was broken. In the same year a separate Parliament was provided for Northern Ireland in Belfast, but Northern Ireland, whose political character is based on Protestant settlements from the seventeenth century onwards, remained very firmly a part of the United Kingdom and retained its representation at Westminster. Between 1801 and 1918, the fundamental preoccupation of the bulk of the Irish members in the House of Commons was to restore self-government to Ireland. With the emergence of Charles Stewart Parnell as its leader in 1874, the Irish Party became a tightly organised group of some eighty members, expert in parliamentary procedure, which they used, to considerable advantage, to block any business that did not advance their cause.

In 1881 the Irish Nationalists helped to prolong a sitting of the House of Commons for nearly two days. The government's purpose had been to get the leave of the House to bring in the Protection of Persons and

Property Bill, designed to coerce political opponents in Ireland. The sitting was ended by Speaker Brand who, on his own authority, proposed that the motion to bring in the bill should be voted upon at once. He "closured" the debate. Until that moment, no one had had power in the House of Commons to end a debate so long as any member still wished to speak; and when the Speaker acted as he did, some Irish Nationalist members were still eager to continue the debate, or rather to delay the moment when the government was permitted to bring in a bill which to them was detestable.

The Speaker's unprecedented intervention was warmly supported by the Prime Minister (Liberal) and the Leader of the opposition (Conservative), and in 1882 the closure of debates was authorised in a standing order of the House. The Irish Nationalists continued their campaign of obstruction by other means, and in 1887, when another Irish coercion bill was before the House of Commons, a Conservative government, with the tacit assent of the Liberal opposition, introduced the first "guillotine" motion: a timetable for the ending of the committee stage of a bill. Morley, in his *Life of Gladstone*,[1] described this motion as "the most remarkable innovation upon parliamentary rule and practice since Cromwell and Colonel Pride". (Colonel Pride "purged" the House of Commons of members objectionable to the Cromwellians in 1648, and Cromwell dissolved the Long Parliament in 1653.) The closure and the guillotine have remained in the armoury of successive governments ever since and both are used from time to time—by Labour as well as Conservative governments—to speed the passage of business.

The only recent proposal to introduce into the House of Commons as a group of members with as distinctive a national interest as that of Southern Irish was made in 1955. The British delegates to a Malta round-table conference recommended that the Maltese should be directly represented in the House of Commons at Westminster, and that Malta should be integrated with the United Kingdom. The proposal has so far come to nothing, but if it is ever put into effect it will mean the arrival at Westminster of a group of members who have no principal concern with the affairs of the United Kingdom. There would be fewer Maltese members than there were Irish Nationalists, and to that extent it would not be easy for Maltese members, if they were so minded, to hold up the normal business of the House of Commons.

With the departure of the Irish Nationalists, and the failure of the Maltese to arrive, the House of Commons has been able, since 1921, to pursue its course of making changes by consent. There is another great advantage of the parliamentary system. It tends to produce stable government. The governments of 1924-29, 1931-35, 1935-45, 1945-50, 1955-59 and of 1959 onwards could all rely on substantial majorities in the House of Commons. None of these governments was threatened with defeat, except in 1940 in circumstances which were abnormal. Executive power was ample and a government's firmness in pursuing policies broadly acceptable to the party which supported it was limited only by its vision and competence.

So long as the government is chosen from the majority party in the House of Commons, and so long as that majority is large enough to guarantee the government's security, after allowing for the protests of small groups of dissenters, for sickness and for absence abroad, there is no inherent defect in the British parliamentary system to prevent strong government. Action may, of course, be slower than it could be in a dictatorship. The parliamentary processes involve argument, debates, votes and public inquiries before executive or administrative action is finally authorised. But the disadvantages of delay are far outweighed by the ultimate general assent to the changes made—or, if not assent, a willingness to abandon resistance on the ground that the case against a particular proposal has been fully stated and at least considered. When public opinion as a whole recognises that a national emergency has arisen, the parties in Parliament agree to grant exceptional powers to the government—on a temporary basis. In such circumstances, the government can act as quickly and radically as any other in the world.

A British government resting on an ample majority in the House of Commons is in a stronger executive position than an administration in the United States, where the constitution was framed deliberately to keep the executive and legislative functions of government separate. The President of the United States possesses in himself greater power than that which rests in the Prime Minister in Britain, but the President's administration may be hampered by a hostile or sceptical Congress: no British government would be similarly handicapped if it rested on an adequate majority in the House of Commons. The President does not fall if his own party is in a minority in Congress: the Prime Minister does, and this fact is a marvellous cohesive in party life.

A third great merit of the British parliamentary system is that it offers a rapid means of revealing folly, extravagance, corruption, or high-handedness wherever they may be found in the conduct of governments, parties or individuals. Over the years, an elaborate set of rules has been devised to prevent a reckless use of the power to question ministers, but power remains to challenge the government on some urgent matter of public importance at a few hours' notice.

In the case of individuals, each member of the House of Commons is held to be responsible for the statements he makes. The conduct of an individual member, or his statements, may be challenged by another member. There is a right of reply in the form of a "personal statement" by the member challenged, and this cannot be debated. Thus, by a process of dialectics, the truth may emerge; and the question-hour with which the proceedings of the House of Commons open on four days of each week is, at its best, an educational battle of wits from which the public may judge the merits of the rival parties and their champions.

These, then, are the three principal merits of the British parliamentary system: the ability to introduce radical, if not revolutionary, changes by consent; the establishment of stable government; and the rapid checking of abuse. What are the disadvantages?

The chief defect of the system is that it produces a House of Commons that is unrepresentative of the differences of political opinion within the country as a whole. Minority groups within the larger parties, or constituting separate parties themselves, tend to be squeezed out of representation in the House of Commons proportionate to their total vote in the country. Independent candidates, without the backing of any party organisation, have had virtually no chance of being elected since the university seats were abolished at the general election of 1950. The effect of the system may be seen by comparing Tables I and II (p. 27). In 1945, taking the total poll, approximately 30,500 votes secured the return of one Labour member, 47,000 votes secured the return of one Conservative, and 183,000 votes secured the return of one Liberal. The electoral system which has been in force since 1950, and which, with relatively minor differences, had been operating for many years previously, gives the victory to the candidate with the highest number of votes, whether or not his majority over the next most successful candidate exceeds the sum of his rivals' votes. The elector can express no preference in his ballot paper for a second candidate, and, since 1950, there has been no constituency in which more than one candidate could be elected. As a result, a Conservative may win a constituency in which there is a large anti-Conservative majority as represented by the combined Labour, Liberal and perhaps Communist polls; and a Labour candidate may win a constituency in which there is a large anti-socialist majority (Conservative and Liberal).

The voting system favours a contest between the two most powerful parties in the country. The third parties have only a small chance of winning a seat. This situation is naturally resented by the Liberals who advocate electoral reform so that their total vote in the country may be proportionately represented by seats in the House of Commons. John Stuart Mill claimed that no form of representation was truly democratic unless all minorities were represented in it according to their strength in the country. In 1884 the Proportional Representation Society was formed in Britain to advocate a change in the electoral system. Several methods of proportional representation exist, but there is space here to mention only those constituencies in the United Kingdom where members have been elected to the House of Commons by proportional representation since the end of the second world war. Universities which elected two or more members in 1945 conducted their ballots on the principle of the single transferable vote, whereby the elector indicates the order in which he would place each of the candidates. If the number of first preferences for any one candidate exceeds a stated quota, that candidate has been elected, and lower preferences are then taken into account.

The election of two "burgesses" for Cambridge University in 1945 illustrates the process. The candidates were Mr (later Sir) Kenneth Pickthorn, Conservative, who was then President of Corpus Christi College, Cambridge; Mr Wilson Harris, Independent, who was then editor of the *Spectator*; Mr J. B. Priestley, Independent, novelist and playwright; Dr Charles Hill, Independent (later Lord Hill of Luton), who was then secretary of the British Medical Association, and later became a minister in Conservative governments; and Air Commodore Howard-Williams, Independent, who was then air correspondent of the *Daily Telegraph*. On the first count, the preferences put the candidates in this order: 1 Pickthorn, 2 Priestley, 3 Harris, 4 Hill, 5 Howard-Williams. Pickthorn's first preferences exceeded the quota and he was elected "senior burgess' for the University. A second member had to be found. After transferring second, third and fourth preferences, Wilson Harris was elected with Priestley runner-up. In the Scottish Universities' election in 1945, the candidate who was bottom of the poll on first preferences was elected one of the three members for his constituency on the third count. Since the university seats were abolished at Westminster, proportional representation has been retained for the election of four members for Queen's University, Belfast, in the Northern Ireland Parliament. At a general election in 1962 three counts were made before all four members for Queen's University had been elected.

The method of election is not the only factor which makes the House of Commons less than completely representative of political opinion in the country. While the expenses which may be incurred by any candidate during an election campaign are strictly limited by law, the organisation of a constituency for party purposes involves expense and the services both of professional and voluntary workers. Election campaigns are fought on national programmes with the backing of the parties' national headquarters which are costly to maintain.

The effect of all this is to give a candidate who is endorsed by an organised party at least a technical advantage over other candidates. The process of endorsement is thus at the heart of the electoral process. Methods differ in the various parties, but the first stage—the selection of a candidate by a constituency party—is common to the Conservative, Labour and Liberal Parties and normally is decisive. The members of a party in a constituency generally nominate a selection committee to interview possible candidates. Someone is chosen: usually a man, for women candidates do not greatly attract selectors. The individual selected is recommended for adoption by the constituency party, and, as a rule, is adopted if the national headquarters have no objection.

Inevitably, constituency parties are run by their most active members who, in the case of the Labour Party, tend to be the left of centre, and in the case of the Conservative Party to the right of centre. A candidate may therefore emerge who is the preference of an activist group, but so long as he is the official party candidate all sections of the party will be urged to vote for him. Endorsement by a party's national headquarters is a check upon extremism: the Conservatives have withdrawn official support from a candidate, selected by a constituency party, who was thought to be near-fascist; Labour will not endorse candidates who are thought to be too close to communism; and the Liberals have formally disowned a candidate who advertised himself as a Liberal candidate but whose views on the colour problem were far to the right of those of official Liberalism. The effect of this system is that a candidate may be elected to the House of Commons whose political opinions are shared only by a minority of those who voted for him: a majority may have supported him only as the official candidate of a national party with which they broadly agreed.

Even if one were to assume that the individuals who composed the House of Commons represented between them a fair sample of opinion in the country, their opportunity to express differences of opinion in the House of Commons is nonetheless limited by practices dictated by the needs of party politics. Party members are controlled by officers of their respective parties ("Whips") whose task it is to see that the proposals of the government, or the decisions of the opposition, are supported by the votes of their party members in the House of Commons. Elaborate machinery exists to prevent members of the government or leaders of the opposition from being out of touch with the prevailing views of their respective supporters. But, when an issue comes to the vote, loyalty can be demanded under threat of political sanctions. The sense in which members are expected to vote may be, and generally is, approved by majorities in the parties concerned, but there can still be considerable and vigorous minority groups whose differences from the official line cannot be effectively expressed except at the risk of punishment.

The Whips have not arrived by accident. The system is not secret, except that the words spoken by a Chief Whip to bring a recalcitrant member to heel are not normally made known. The public is aware of party discipline, which, though it is often condemned by commentators as stifling individual conscience and freedom of mind and thus impoverishing the quality of British politics, has not so far provoked an irresistible demand for its abolition. In fact, party discipline is accepted as part of the alternative government system on the ground that, if there is essential political work to be done, it should be done effectively. This is taken to mean that a party applying a programme for which the electors gave it authority, or a party resisting policies which its supporters dislike, should be able to act at all times quickly and with maximum strength. The fragmentation of parties, which the British find in the parliamentary history of France, is seen by many loyal party workers as a short-cut to chaos. Party discipline is at its most oppressive when applied to secure support for some new decision to meet circumstances which had not been foreseen in any election programme. Any government must at times appeal to its supporters to trust its judgment; any opposition may have to make a quick reaction which its supporters have had little time to consider in detail.

There are other criticisms of the parliamentary system as it now works. Chief of these is the claim that the government of the day, and particularly the Prime Minister with his ultimate sanction of seeking a new general election, are growing in power at the expense of Parliament. This claim is based both on the complexity of modern government—the need for decisions on issues, such as the use of nuclear power or the exploration of space, which can only be taken with expert advice that is not generally available—and on the inadequate equipment of members of Parliament to challenge the government effectively. The power of the government in relation to Parliament is increased further by the growing web of international commitments which tend to limit national sovereignty and bind the country to decisions in which other countries share and which cannot easily be set aside. It takes a sharp mind to recognise, when Britain's membership of some new international body is being approved, all the future commitments which may follow. Some members of the House of Commons were shocked to discover in 1962 that Britain's membership of Western European Union, created in 1955, limited Parliament's ability to control some of the defence arrangements proposed by the Union. The more Britain's position in the world compels her to act with other states

—and the more the process gains momentum—the less Parliament will be able to control the government except on the broadest issues such as the decision whether or not to make a new commitment.

The change in the position of governments and prime ministers may be exaggerated. Queen Victoria in 1880 was most anxious to avoid inviting Gladstone, whom she disliked, to form a government. She first invited someone else, who failed to secure the support he needed. Gladstone had perforce to be given the task— and succeeded. A prime minister who comes to power in such circumstances is in a position of formidable strength. Similarly, it can be argued that the House of Commons is in no worse position now, when discovering the ramifications of international commitments, than it was in 1914 when Parliament (and many members of the Liberal government) learnt for the first time, at the approach to the first world war, of Britain's secret engagements to France.

The question of the adequacy of members of the House of Commons to check the executive is often debated. Is Parliament attracting men and women of the quality who used to be there? If not, why not? There is no lack of candidates for selection in vacant constituencies. When Churchill announced in 1963 that he would not stand again for election at Woodford, Essex, a hundred Conservatives applied for selection in his place. (Woodford is an attractive seat—near London and within easy reach of Westminster.)

The disadvantages of service in the House of Commons has been widely advertised: an effective salary of £1,750 a year which members, with no other source of income, find inadequate to meet essential expenses; lack of facilities for secretarial work and for meetings with constituents; lack of expert advice to permit members to examine government action thoroughly, particularly in the more technical fields such as defence; and lack of opportunity to speak in debate. These disadvantages do not weigh equally heavily on all. A member may do more or less work according to his ability and temperament. There is no doubt, however, that from time to time members on both sides of the House of Commons see themselves as no more than "votes" for or against the government, and suffer from the frustration of feeling that they have little part in the formation of policy.

Some members also feel themselves hampered by the means of communication with the public. Since the beginning of this century, the amount of space given in the newspapers to reports of Parliament has declined. This is true of all newspapers. Even if a member of the House of Commons is lucky enough to be called on to speak in debate, his speech may be condensed to a report of only a few lines in the press, or may not be mentioned at all. Every member's speech is, of course, reported in full in the Official Report, Hansard, and copies of Hansard are sent by members to individuals in their constituencies. But this record does not reach anything like the number of readers (electors) whom the member wishes to influence. Broadcasting has provided a new means of mass-communication, but this, too, is not regarded by all members as completely satisfactory; for the broadcasting authorities, the British Broadcasting Corporation and the Independent Television Authority, must inevitably select the members who are put on the air so long as parliamentary debates are not broadcast. Those who are not selected, for technical rather than political reasons, have a grievance. By the end of 1963 the campaign for televising debates from Parliament had gained considerable support.

Yet, despite shorter press reports and the selectivity of the broadcasting authorities, more people in the country know more about what is happening in Parliament than ever before. The decline in the space given to Parliamentary affairs in the newspapers has been accompanied, since 1900, by a great increase in newspaper circulation. The development of press techniques has led to a concentration of attention on whatever news items are thought by the newspapers to be of first-class importance and Parliamentary news in this category cannot be missed by any reader.

So, too, broadcasting has brought parliamentary news into millions of homes, and indeed the scope of broadcasts on social, political and industrial affairs is constantly widening. Television viewers may see for themselves what a leading politician looks like when he is talking. The annual conferences of the political parties and of the Trades Union Congress are reported at length in broadcasts. So powerfully does television appeal to public figures as a means of mass communication that it might become regarded as an alternative to Parliament. Politics could be conducted almost as a radio plebiscite. Parliament is aware of this danger, which is resisted largely because an opposition is always suspicious that a government might seek too large a share of broadcasting time.

One further criticism of the parliamentary system must be recorded. Some observers believe that the seat of power, which once lay in Parliament, has moved outside and is now shared by interests inadequately represented there, such as the great industrial corporations and the trade unions with their vast economic strength. The trade unions provide the Labour Party with most of its income, but their attitude to politics is becoming more detached. They are almost invariably consulted directly by the government on industrial affairs. Their spokesmen can make the unions' case to the Prime Minister and all subordinate ministers. The access of the unions to the government has been made steadily easier since 1939 and is now unimpeded. As a result, it has become less important, in the unions' views, that their case should be managed by Labour politicians in the House of Commons. The unions have discouraged their leading officials from standing for election to the House of Commons. In 1945, for example, an official of the National Union of General and Municipal Workers, Mr (later Sir) Thomas Williamson, was elected Labour Member of Parliament for Brigg. In 1946 he was appointed general secretary of his union and was compelled by his union to choose between service in Parliament and his continuance as general secretary: in 1948, he resigned his parliamentary seat.

The attractions of the business world are different. Big business may offer a man a far greater financial reward than he can get from politics, even as a minister, and can give him a sharper sense of direct power. Lord Boyd of Merton and Lord Chandos are instances of men who resigned from high office in Conservative governments to take up careers in business. The contrast in the scales of income open to business men and to politicians was shown to the public when, in 1961, Dr Beeching, the technical director of Imperial Chemical Industries, one of the largest commercial concerns in Britain, accepted the chairmanship of the British Transport Commission, a state enterprise which controlled the railway system among other activities. Dr Beeching agreed to become chairman of the Commission on condition that he continued to be paid the salary he had been receiving from Imperial Chemical Industries: £24,000 a year. This is by far the largest salary paid to the chairman of any nationalised undertaking. (The Prime Minister's salary is £10,000, of which £4,000 is free of tax.)

Concentrations of financial and industrial power

outside Parliament are watched sharply by members of the House of Commons, but the extent to which they rival Parliament in control of the country's affairs may be exaggerated. Broadly, the Labour Party, with its close ties with the trade union movement, acts naturally in sympathy with the unions; and the Conservatives understand and appreciate the interests of the business world. It is probably true to say that the House of Commons has only been the seat of political and economic power in those periods when the landowners controlled politics and were the chief capitalists in the state. The Reform Bill of 1832, which opened the House of Commons to the representatives of the new men of the Industrial Revolution, was the start of an era when power began to spread not only to the machine men, but to the workers whom they employed.

All the defects in the parliamentary system do not outweigh its advantages. Parliament can, as Labour discovered in 1945, effect a social revolution. It gives effect to the wishes of millions of electors. The party in power cannot act for long against the determined opposition of its own supporters, or of a majority of electors in the country; and the system guarantees that if the government of the day forfeits majority support it can be replaced by another with no great disturbance of the nation's life.

IV

THE POLITICAL PARTIES

THE principal political parties in Britain are organised to gain power through the election of a majority of members in the House of Commons. The Conservative, Labour and Liberal parties are all committed to the parliamentary democratic system as now practised in Britain. There are other parties which seek power but which have so far made little appeal to the electors. The British Communist Party has secured representation in the House of Commons since it was founded in 1920, but there have never been more than two Communists in the House of Commons at any one time, and since 1950 there has been none. The Communists, therefore, have sought power elsewhere, and particularly through the trade union movement. The Union Movement, a fascist organisation, is another political group which has failed to attract the electors. It seeks support by a joint appeal to national pride and national fear, and tries to turn the existence of minority groups within the community into a source of national discontent and thus into a means of increasing the power of the Union Movement.

The Communist Party and the Union Movement would gain most in a revolutionary situation when widespread and passionate unrest might lead to a demand for the overthrow of the existing system of government and its replacement by some authoritarian system. Both groups are thwarted by the flexibility of the parties represented in Parliament. Henry James, in *The Portrait of a Lady*, puts into the mouth of one of his characters, an American, this account of Britain and the British:

> It's a very fine country on the whole—finer perhaps than we give it credit for on the other side. There are several improvements I should like to see introduced; but the necessity of them doesn't seem to be generally felt as yet. When the necessity of a thing is generally felt they usually manage to accomplish it; but they seem to feel pretty comfortable about waiting till then.[1]

Since the relatively spacious days of the 'eighties, much has happened to sharpen the public sense of the necessity for change in Britain, but it has remained true that "they usually manage to accomplish it".

To understand the ability of Britain to adapt herself to a new rôle in the world, it is essential to know what the political parties are really like. The conditions of party warfare inevitably obscure the virtues which a party may possess and over-emphasise its defects, but it is a reasonable assumption that any party which secures the election of members to the House of Commons has convinced some voters—in the case of the Conservative and Labour parties, many millions of voters—that it possesses virtues which meet a national need. To the faithful Labour voter, all Conservatives seem "wicked". To the faithful Conservative, all Labour candidates are "dangerous Reds". To Labour and Conservative voters alike, the Liberals are "unrealistic"; and the Liberal voter regards the two larger parties as the upper and nether millstones which grind to nothing man's most precious quality—his individuality. The rich and aristocratic Lord Rosebery, who became a Liberal prime minister, wrote of the Tories in 1870 that "they would call themselves communists to get seats, but when they have got them they are as illiberal as ever". The Communists regard the lot as being at best mindless, and at worst unscrupulous exploiters of the poor and defenceless for their own selfish ends.

THE CONSERVATIVE PARTY

The Conservative Party has a persisting unity denied both to the Labour and Liberal Parties. Its main purpose never changes: to preserve, so long as may be, a state of society in which private property and private enterprise may flourish. They believe that these are the foundations of economic health. They proclaim this view. It is shared by millions of voters. Labour and the Liberals are federations of groups of people with differing interests but all in favour of some changes. These parties are therefore less coherent than the Conservatives. But the great strength of the Conservative Party, which has made it an invaluable element in the development of British politics, has been its willingness to compromise, to save what it can of its private world by making concessions to public demands fostered by the work of its rivals (and sometimes indeed by the campaigns of individual Conservatives). The explanation of the Conservatives' resilience lies in Disraeli's definition of Conservative aims: "The preservation of our institutions, the maintenance of our empire, and the amelioration of the condition of our people."

The Conservatives are a "constitutional" party. They support the Crown, the peers (spiritual and temporal) and the Commons. The "peers spiritual" are those Archbishops and Bishops of the Established (and protestant) Church of England who sit in the House of Lords. Yet a party committed to defend the established order has introduced radical changes in British politics. Con-

servative champions of the Church of England introduced
the Catholic Emancipation Bill (1829). The leader of the
party that rested on the support of the great landowners,
who drew their wealth from agriculture, repealed the
Corn Laws (1846) and opened an era of free trade to the
great advantage of the industrial manufacturers. The
party which rested on privilege introduced a great extension to the franchise in 1867, raising the number of voters
from 1.3 million to 2.2 million. Lord Derby, who was
then Prime Minister and was one of the great landowners
of the country, said of this reform: "No doubt we are
making a great experiment and taking a leap in the dark;
but I have the greatest confidence in the sound sense of
my fellow-countrymen, and I entertain a strong hope
that the extended franchise which we are now conferring
upon them will be the means of placing the institutions
of this country on a firmer basis." This plain statement
of one of the principles of Conservative conduct can be
taken as a guide to much that has happened since.

Three elements combine to keep the Conservative
Party in movement and to save it, except at intervals,
from the perils of rigidity. The party relies more than
Labour or the Liberals on the judgment of its leaders who
have retained, in the party's structure, a dominant position. Conservative leaders over decades have been principally concerned to discover how quickly and completely
they can share their sense of future events with the
party's rank and file, and how far it has been safe, both
in the national and party interest, to apply those policies
for which the more ardent party workers yearn. In this
double rôle of seers and worldlings, Conservative leaders
have had to teach and restrain; for Conservative supporters, more than Labour or Liberal followers, feel the
strength of their position rather than defend it by argument. Labour and the Liberals are great arguers.

The second element is the nature of the men and

women who become Conservative Members of Parliament. They are for the most part quite ordinary men and women who know their constituencies inside out. Conservative politicians are pictured by their rivals either as greedy capitalists or as playboys: highly born, rich, elegant, agreeably stupid and dangerously well-mannered because they live so far above the common world. A few Conservatives belong to these two types but they are outnumbered in the House of Commons by those of middle or lower middle class origin. The solemn Conservative politician—and there are plenty of them—is very solemn indeed, priggish almost. No Marxist could be more opinionated or more dedicated to the support of his own party.

The only man in the House of Commons who is a member of the Electrical Trades Union, one of the most highly skilled of Britain's unions, is the Conservative member for Totnes, Ray Mawby. He was formerly a shop steward in a factory and president of the Rugby branch of his union. It would have seemed natural for a member of this union to have been elected to Parliament on the Labour side. Labour has intimate links with the trade union movement which will be described later, and with two exceptions the trade unionists in the House of Commons are all Labour members. Mr Mawby is a special case. The Conservatives have long claimed, with truth, that very many trade unionists—perhaps some millions —vote Conservative. The party wished, therefore, to get a trade unionist adopted as a Conservative candidate and elected. Ray Mawby was chosen for a safe Conservative seat in Devonshire, Totnes, and was elected in 1955 with a majority of 11,594 over Labour and Liberal opponents. In 1959 he increased his majority to 13,809 over Labour and Liberal opponents.

At the time of his first election the Electrical Trades Union was controlled by the Communists. They gained a majority on the union's executive shortly after the second world war and kept it until 1961. The Conservatives therefore had the special satisfaction of sending to Parliament a man who belonged to the "Reddest" union in the country. Mawby entered Macmillan's government in March 1963 as Assistant Postmaster General. He has remained a token. Few Conservative associations have been willing to adopt trade unionists as candidates; they prefer more conventional representatives of their party. The only other Conservative member who is a trade unionist is J. C. Jennings, of Burton-on-Trent, a member of the National Union of Teachers and a former schoolmaster. When Parliament is concerned with the interests of this union, which is composed mainly of teachers in state schools rather than of those in independent schools which charge fees, the Conservative member for Burton-on-Trent normally acts with other members of the National Union of Teachers in the House who are all on the Labour side. The isolation of these two trade unionists among the Conservative members is obvious, but it would be easy to miss the political reality that the Conservative Party attracts large, not to say massive, support from industrial workers in the organised trade unions.

The third element is the electorate itself. A party that polled 14,000,000 votes in 1959 cannot be out of touch with popular opinion. It cannot be regarded by so large a section of the community as an archaic and aristocratic institution seeking only to preserve the wealth and privileges of the few. On the other hand, the rich and privileged trust the Conservative Party to go to the safety limit in upholding the established order. Thus the Conservatives draw strength from the privileged and from millions of others who see no objection in becoming privileged if it can be done. This double support gives continuing vigour to a party of the right and so reduces the danger of extreme reaction. The persistence in Britain of a moderate, flexible, constitutional party of the right is one of the main safeguards of parliamentary democracy.

The Conservatives are supported by men of property and members of established institutions—the Church, the Law, the armed forces, the learned professions—and by mass opinion which supports these institutions. Individual members of all these institutions belong to other parties, but the predominant tone of such institutions is Conservative. The history of the university constituencies in Britain before their abolition in 1950 shows plainly the conservatism of the academic world: the conservatism, that is, of the graduates who had a vote but not necessarily that of the undergraduates who had none. The universities never sent a Labour member to Parliament: they chose Conservatives mainly, sometimes Liberals and sometimes "Independents" who might be more or less conservative. Even the Nonconformist Protestant churches, which at the turn of the century were predominantly Liberal and radical, are to a growing extent finding their political outlet through the Conservative Party as being, in their view, the only practical alternative to a Labour Party which they regard as less committed to Christianity than the Conservative Party. (This view is hotly contested by Christian Socialists who see the Conservative Party as a Temple of Mammon.)

Andrew Roth, in his reference book, *The Business Background of Members of Parliament*,[2] states that eight out of ten Conservatives had "substantial present or past business connections". The comparable figures he gives for the other parties are almost one in three for the Liberals and almost one in four for Labour. But the mass appeal of the Conservative Party must not be forgotten: it can be overlooked when the party, judged from its representation in the House of Commons, is seen from a selected view point.

Twice the Conservative Party has recruited itself from the Liberals. Joseph Chamberlain, a radical reformer in local government, separated himself from Gladstone, the Liberal leader, in 1886, because he could not accept the Liberal policy of Home Rule for Ireland, which was then part of the United Kingdom. In 1895 Chamberlain accepted office in a Conservative government, and his followers, known as "Liberal Unionists"—"union", that is, between Britain and Ireland—became virtually absorbed into the Conservative Party. (The principal organisation of Conservative supporters to-day is still officially called the National Union of Conservative and Unionist Associations.) Chamberlain was also an ardent imperialist, and carried with him into the Conservative camp some but not all of the Liberals who shared his imperialist dream.

Again, in 1931, a section of the Liberal Party led by Sir John Simon (later Lord Simon) abandoned the traditional Liberal policy of free trade for that of protection in a period of heavy unemployment, and were pressed into the Conservative mould although retaining the form of independent political life as Liberal Nationals (now called National Liberals). There are to-day 21 National Liberals in the House of Commons. They are indistinguishable from Conservatives in their actions, but their party label is still a nuisance (as the Conservatives intended that it should be) to the independent Liberal Party.

Conservatives suffer from two faults which from time to time divert the party from the broad stream of national feeling. They persuade themselves that they are the true Englishmen, and that members of other parties are either negligible outsiders or dangerous revolutionaries. The Conservative, in his most exalted moments, identifies himself with membership of the Church of England, service in the armed forces, devotion to the

Crown, and dedicated defence of private property. He sees himself as a patriot. He will give all he has got—his life, certainly—for a patriotic cause. But, as happened during two world wars, he will find himself at the point of danger with other Britons—from other parties. The Conservative sometimes misses the point that service to one's country may take different forms. The history of the 1945 general election shows how the British public may be offended by the arrogance of the Conservatives when they claim a monopoly of the national spirit.

The second defect is a tendency to overstate the claims of private property and privilege, to defend these institutions beyond the limits of social health, and to underestimate the extent to which individuals may be willing to subordinate personal advantage to the benefit of the community as a whole.

This is the defect of a virtue: an earthy sense of the ordinary man's interest in his "bread and butter". A vivid example of this tendency was given by the Conservative Chancellor of the Exchequer, Selwyn Lloyd,[3] in his Budget speech of April 17, 1961. He exempted from liability to surtax, which is levied in addition to income tax, all those whose gross earned income was less than £5,000 a year. This change became effective on January 1, 1963. In making this concession, Lloyd said:

> Surtax begins at £2,000. This figure was fixed in 1920. There is force in the argument against the present level of surtax. In the modern world the work of the manager, the scientist, the technologist, is of increased importance not only to himself but to the community. In other countries there are much higher rewards for individual effort and skill. Therefore I want to do what I can to ensure that the present incidence of surtax does not act as a disincentive to those who have positions of responsi-

bility in our industries and elsewhere in our national life.'

The debate on the Budget continued for several days, and Selwyn Lloyd spoke again on April 20. He dealt with the criticsm made by Labour members that the Budget, and in particular the surtax relief, would make the rich richer.

I think they are out of date, said Lloyd. A man who is earning £5,000 gross is not rich unless he has large private means as well. No doubt, forty or fifty years ago on that sort of income, one could have had a house in London, a house in the country, a large domestic staff, and still have been able to save. But to-day, a man earning £5,000 gross, unless he has private means, has the greatest difficulty in providing out of his income for the education of his family and for saving. That is a fact of life, and surtax for him, unless he has private means, is at present penal.⁵

All that Lloyd said was true—but he did not tell the whole political truth. He was correct in contrasting the real value of an income of £5,000 to-day with what it had been in 1920. He was correct in mentioning the scarcity of "large domestic staffs" as a sign of the decline in the standard of living of some members of the community. He was correct in speaking of the growth of the group of scientists, technicians and business executives in Britain who come within the £2,000-£5,000 a year income bracket. He was correct in saying there was little margin for saving, especially if the income earner chose to pay fees for the education of his children. Without question, Lloyd was offering a benefit to a section of the community most of whom might be expected to support the Conservative Party.

Yet his concession was attacked on several grounds. He was accused of benefiting surtax payers in a period when the government was preaching wage restraint in general. He was accused of ignoring the fact that millions of wage earners regarded an annual income of £5,000 a year as wealth. In the year which ended on March 31, 1961, the Commissioners of Inland Revenue reported that out of 20,383,000 incomes in Britain, only 156,000 were between £3,000 and £5,000 a year; nearly two million people earned too little to pay any income tax at all. Lloyd was reminded that each wage earner might apply to himself the argument in favour of incentives for the "valuable" members of the community.

Selwyn Lloyd's acceptance of the 1920 value of an income of £5,000 brought into question the economic health of the country at that time, when instability led to a social upheaval. His acceptance of current Conservative standards was also questioned. Why should he assume, it was asked, that a man whose income was £5,000 a year should prefer to pay fees for the education of his children instead of using the state school system? He was accused of trying to perpetuate educational privilege which the state system had not yet effectively challenged.

The sharpest criticism of Selwyn Lloyd's concession to the surtax payer was that it cost the Exchequer a large sum of money which could have been spent—if there were economic justification for spending so large a sum in the circumstances which then prevailed—to better purpose, for example in greater benefits to old-age pensioners. The relief to surtax payers was estimated to deny the Exchequer a revenue of £58 million in 1962-63 and of £83 million in 1963-64, the first full year of its application.

Conservatives warmly approved of Lloyd's concession. They were not moved by the argument that the relief could have been more advantageously used. They wanted this relief for the surtax payer whom they saw as the creator of more national wealth. In any case, his proposal was part of the Conservatives' plan to redistribute the national wealth in favour of those who, since 1939, had lost a larger part of their incomes in direct taxation than any other section of the community.

THE LABOUR PARTY

The Labour Party is a federation of different interests with the common purpose of helping the underdog, of improving the standard of life of the poorer members of the community so that no one shall suffer from the effects of artificial disabilities. This definition of the main purpose of the Labour Party may seem too simple, but it explains why the history of the party has seemed erratic when judged by the standards of continental socialist parties which have tended to be more systematic than Labour. When Labour supporters in Britain were divided upon the challenge to the party leaders made by Aneurin Bevan and his followers in 1950 and for some time afterwards, observers who had been brought up in the tradition of continental socialism could not understand what the fuss was about. To them, Bevan seemed scarcely more fierce or doctrinaire a socialist than the leaders whose gradualism he was attacking.

The very naming of the party—a stroke of genius in British politics—indicates the variety of its composition. A "Labour" party can attract support from all who work for a living whether or not they are dedicated marxists or socialists. The name does not of itself frighten the more timorous or prosperous income earners who might recoil from support of a "Workers'" Party or a "Socialist" Party. The Conservatives have for long realised the appeal of the name "Labour", and in consequence consistently refer to its members as "socialists".

The strictly socialist content of Labour's objectives is defined in Clause Four of the party's constitution which includes this paragraph: "To secure for the workers by hand or brain the full fruits of their industry and the most equitable distribution thereof that may be possible, upon the basis of the common ownership of the means of production, distribution and exchange, and the best obtainable system of popular administration and control of each industry or service."

This formula was drafted by Sidney Webb (later Lord Passfield) and adopted by the Labour Party Conference in February 1918 as part of a new constitution drawn up by Arthur Henderson, who was then secretary of the Party, with the help of Sidney Webb. The formula still remains part of Labour's constitution although the Labour Party Conference of 1959 was invited by the then leader, Hugh Gaitskell, to "modernise" the statement of the party's objects. It is essential when estimating the impact of the Labour Party on British politics to-day to see Labour's socialism in perspective. Sidney Webb, with his wife, Beatrice, managed the Fabian Society which had been founded in London in 1883 to advocate the application of socialism by degrees. This gradualism was attacked by the more ardent socialists; but the Fabians were willing at one stage to try to make their ideas permeate to the Liberal and Conservative Parties, which then alternated in office, if this process could advance their aims. Arthur Henderson had himself been a member of Lloyd George's war-time Coalition government (predominantly Liberal and Conservative) from August 1916 to August 1917. He was a nonconformist and had entered the Labour Party as a trade unionist. It was only later that he became a socialist. He was almost the ideal type of the solid, honest working man whose word, once given, was trusted absolutely by all who had to deal with him. Webb, the gradualist, and Henderson, the practical trade unionist, persuaded the Labour Conference to accept the clause four formula on socialism.

Emanuel Shinwell, the Labour member for Easington, who has given a lifetime to the service of his party, comments in his book, *The Labour Story*,[6] that this historic paragraph gave Labour a socialist aim which Keir Hardie, first leader of the Parliamentary Labour Party, and other pioneers of the Labour movement "would have regarded as wildly unacceptable to any trade unionist. By 1918 the famous clause four was a reason for enthusiasm about the brave new world once peace had come." Henry Pelling writes of Labour's adoption of the 1918 constitution, including Clause Four:

> The party was thus equipped with a greatly improved constitution, at least for the purpose of making an appeal to the electors as a whole rather than just to the interests of the unions. It also had a practical programme which in domestic affairs was a compromise between Marxian socialism on the one hand and the piecemeal social reform of the (Joseph) Chamberlain-Lloyd George type on the other. All this enabled the party to make its bid to rank as an alternative government of the country: a bid that within the first post-war years was to prove unexpectedly successful.[7]

It may seem a strange claim that the constitution of 1918 should have strengthened Labour's "appeal to the electors as a whole". The constitution reasserted Labour's alliance with the trade unions, introduced the socialist formula, and gave some new power to constituency party representatives who tended to be the more militant socialists within the party. (The power of the constituency representatives was increased in 1937.) These three elements in Labour's make-up have been sharply attacked by Conservatives and Liberals in recent years in the hope of discouraging the electors from giving Labour a second period of power comparable with that of 1945-50. But the 1918 constitution brought into better balance the various interests which had co-operated to form the party in 1900, and, by lessening the appearance of Labour as the party mainly of the industrial workers, broadened its appeal.

The origin of the party is directly relevant to its position to-day. In 1899, the Trades Union Congress adopted by 546,000 votes to 434,000 a resolution submitted by the Amalgamated Society of Railway Servants (now the National Union of Railwaymen) proposing that a conference should be called to promote the representation of labour in Parliament. Representatives of trade unions, co-operative societies and socialist bodies were to be invited to attend. The special conference met in 1900 and on February 28 formed the Labour Representation Committee with J. Ramsay MacDonald, later to become the first Labour Prime Minister, as secretary. MacDonald was then a member of the Independent Labour Party. The Co-operative movement was unwilling at this stage to support the new venture. After the general election of 1906, in which 29 candidates of the Labour Representation Committee were elected Members of Parliament, the name "Labour Party" was adopted. Ten of the new Labour members had been elected in constituencies where the Committee had made a pact with the Liberals. By no stretch of the imagination could the Labour members of 1906 be regarded as dangerous revolutionaries.

In 1900 the trade unions were by no means solidly socialist. Indeed, many had previously been willing to express themselves politically through support of the Liberal Party, just as to-day the unions in the United States use the two dominant capitalist parties, the Democrats and Republicans, for their own political ends. Three socialist groups assisted at the birth of the Labour Party:

88

the Independent Labour Party (founded in Bradford in 1893) which preached "Socialism in our own time", whether or not this gospel would yield them the power to apply it; the Social Democratic Federation, which was marxist; and the Fabian Society.

Mr Pelling comments: "The charges of socialist control and dictation of the new organisation would certainly have had a great deal of substance if it had not been that the three societies were at odds with one another."[8] The Independent Labour Party was much the most powerful of the three, but it later attacked the Labour Party, which it had done so much to create, for its gradualism. In 1932 the Labour Party Conference disaffiliated the Independent Labour Party, and since the general election of 1950 there have been no members of the Independent Labour Party in the House of Commons. The Social Democratic Federation faded out earlier. The Fabian Society persists as a research group.

The gradualist Labour Party survived, and its moderation in advocating and applying radical social changes through the constitutional processes of Parliament has been second only in importance in the history of British politics to the moderation of the Conservative Party in resisting change. Yet the impact of socialist thought on the Labour Party has been a fundamental influence in its development. It explains why Labour overtook the Liberals, from 1922 onwards, as the instrument of radical reform.

The Liberal attitude to economics differed little from that of the Conservatives except that the Liberals were free traders and the Conservatives were on the verge of becoming protectionists. Both parties were, at the beginning of the century, and still are, capitalist parties committed to the support of individual enterprise. Labour was anti-capitalist, collectivist, and more or less socialist in the spirit of the Webb formula. It offered a real alternative to the economic policies of the other two parties, and it became a going concern well before the British Communist Party was founded in 1920. Moreover, when the public began to realise, after the first world war, how great was the scale of the social and economic problems facing Britain, the cause for state intervention gained strength.

But how do the members of the Labour Party interpret socialism? C. A. R. Crosland, the Labour Member for Grimsby, wrote in *The Future of Socialism*:

> It is obvious enough that socialist thought varies through time, and that different doctrines prevail at different periods. This is as it should be. It is not even surprising that different doctrines should be supported at the same time—Owenism and Chartism, Marxism and Christian Socialism, Fabianism and Guild Socialism; there must always be divergent views on the right emphasis and order of priorities, and these will prevent a uniformity of thought. The trouble is that some of the divergencies are not a matter simply of emphasis or the right priorities. They are fundamental, and the doctrines mutually inconsistent.
>
> Thus Fabian collectivism and Welfare Statism require a view of the State diametrically opposed to the Marxist view. The syndicalist view is anti-collectivist. The Marxist tradition is anti-reformist. Owenism differs fundamentally from Marxism and syndicalism on the class war. Morrisite communes and Socialist Guilds are incompatible with nationalisation: and so on. How then to decide which is the correct scripture? It is, of course, impossible.[9]

These differences have not been a fatal handicap to the Labour Party because its power springs from men and women with a practical turn of mind rather than from theorists. The trade unions, which over decades have given the Labour Party its ballast, financially and politically, were founded to establish rights for working people through combination, to raise their economic and social status, and to protect, in periods of unemployment, any gains that had been made. The worker has the most direct interest in his pay packet and in his hours and conditions of work. Results have proved that he can best protect himself in union with other workers. The case for collective action has therefore been accepted largely as a bread-and-butter matter, irrespective of its place in the philosophy of dialectical materialism, and even though the theorists have played a part in persuading the workers that union is strength. And if collective action is the best course for a worker to take to protect his job, why should it not also be the best method for the state to bring about social change? This is how the argument has run.

Each union began by taking collective action on behalf of its own members and was jealous of its autonomy. Pride of independence was naturally highest in the craft unions. (Union rivalry persists in demarcation disputes to-day.) Some unions were therefore reluctant to commit themselves to the new Labour Representation Committee, but this mood began to change almost at once. Legal judgments at the turn of the century against the unions accelerated the flow of union support for Labour, and periods of unemployment between the two world wars sharpened painfully the differences between the wage earners on the one hand, and the salary earners and capitalists on the other. The Labour Party seemed to many who suffered economic hardship, and to others who were shocked by this suffering, the best available means for altering an economic system which produced such results.

The General Strike of 1926, supported by the Trades

Union Congress, was the result of widespread economic misery. It brought into the Labour movement a middle-class intellectual, Hugh Gaitskell, who was then completing his studies as an economist at Oxford. From 1955 until his death in January 1963, Gaitskell was leader of the Labour Party. He represented another important element in the composition of the party: privileged members of the community who were so disturbed by the social inequalities around them, and so convinced that these inequalities would be perpetuated or intensified by the stimulus which the capitalist system gives to private enterprise, that they joined the Labour Party in an effort to secure a decent life for the mass of the people. Gaitskell's predecessor as leader of the Labour Party, Clement Attlee, whose period as leader lasted from 1935 to 1955, had similarly been led as a young man to join the Labour Party by a sharp sense that capitalist orthodoxy could not remove as quickly as he wished, if at all, the causes of the misery and squalor which he saw about him in the social settlement at which he worked in the East End of London. Attlee, Gaitskell, and many others from a prosperous social background were drawn into the Labour Party primarily as practical reformers.

Christianity, and especially evangelical Christianity, has contributed a characteristic strain to the Labour movement. To-day the Labour Party includes Roman Catholics, members of the Church of England, both high and low, and Nonconformists including some Quakers— the absolute pacifists. It is true that there is a militant agnostic element in the party which created the "Socialist Sunday Schools" as an antidote to religion as "the opium of the people", but Labour's actions cannot be fully understood without allowing for the influence which evangelical Christianity has had in its development. John and Charles Wesley in the eighteenth century carried through a religious revival which caught the imagination of the labouring people and gave them a vision of a better world within the discipline of evangelical rather than hierarchical Christianity. Throughout the nineteenth and early twentieth centuries Wesleyan methodism gave strength to popular movements. The radical Liberals benefited first, but Labour later drew power from this source. Methodism encouraged self-discipline, thrift, temperance and education. Its pulpits, filled often by laymen, were a training ground for public speakers. Its ministry gave many men from poor homes their first systematic intellectual training after an elementary schooling. The Nonconformist theological colleges, some of which provided university arts courses for their students, have given hundreds of young men free academic instruction which would otherwise have been denied them. The brotherhood of man, based on Christian faith, was proclaimed in chapels throughout the country.

"Chapel" versus "Church" (of England) in many towns and villages represented a real social and economic rift; and all the time the life of the chapel was, among other things, giving a new assurance to the under-privileged which more and more expressed itself in a political challenge to the power of the rich and orthodox. Nonconformity was born in protest against the religious system imposed by the powerful and privileged, and its insistence on Christian brotherhood drew together those who suffered from social and economic hardship and who saw the supports of the established order—armed force among them—as barriers to the creation of a New Jerusalem. Nonconformity brought to the Labour Party large numbers of men and women whose chief concerns were with social reform and with pacifism, or at least anti-militarism. At the same time, Nonconformity taught the value of the individual human soul. "The Kingdom of God is within you." This doctrine has worked in the

Labour movement against complete subservience to the state. Labour's interest in social reform has been strengthened by the party's experience of local government: another great educational force for countless men and women who have missed the advantages of a long period of schooling and academic training.

The struggle against power and privilege at home was extended in defence of the under-privileged everywhere. The workers' revolution in Russia in 1917 was hailed as the dawn of a new age, which indeed it was although the character of the age then inaugurated has turned out differently from what had been hoped by many well-wishers in Britain. So, too, Labour has supported the advance to independence of Britain's colonial territories. It has opposed the nazi and fascist dictatorships. Labour based its foreign policy after the first world war on support for the League of Nations and collective security: its foreign policy is now based on support for the United Nations.

The Labour Party is also influenced and helped by the Co-operative movement which operates economically between complete state regulation and private competition. Co-operation, as a system based on the combination of producers and consumers to sell and buy in common and share the profits, made its first mark in Britain when Robert Owen ran his cotton mills at New Lanark in Scotland with success from 1799 to 1822. In 1844, some Lancashire weavers opened the first co-operative shop at Rochdale. To-day the Co-operative movement in the United Kingdom is a vast undertaking. Total sales by retail societies in 1961 were £1,044 million.

Although the co-operators were fearful of losing their identity when the Labour Representation Committee was formed, they now have a firm working arrangement with the Labour Party. The Co-operative Congress founded a political party in 1917, and in 1926 Co-operative parties were allowed to affiliate to constituency Labour parties. In 1941, representatives of the Co-operative Party joined on equal terms with those of the Labour Party and the Trades Union Congress in a National Council of Labour. In 1946 it was agreed between the Labour and Co-operative parties that Co-operative candidates should stand at parliamentary elections as "Labour and Co-operative" candidates, and in 1959 it was further agreed that the number of Co-operative candidates at any election should be limited to thirty. In the 1959 election, sixteen "Labour and Co-operative" candidates were elected to the House of Commons. They act at all times with the Labour members, but there are at times tension between the Labour and Co-operative parties. Co-operative interest in a "vertical" economic structure—the control within a co-operative society of all stages of distribution from producer to consumer—has conflicted with Labour's preference for a "horizontal" structure, for example in the nationalisation of the supply of a particular product.

The democratic organisation of the Co-operative movement—the members of each society elect their own officers—and the size of its annual trade, with its promise of economic power (not so far realised in Britain), have provoked the Communists to attempt to gain control of the movement through assiduous attendance at meetings and the election of their candidates to management committees. This campaign has not yet produced dazzling results for the Communists.

All these different elements in the Labour Party, which have persisted with varying degrees of emphasis since its foundation, compel the leadership as its first task to seek always the largest common measure of agreement in order to give Labour some stability as a national party. Labour cannot afford to be regarded by the public as a collection of cranks: pacifists, vegetarians, animal lovers, cloudy humanitarians and "Reds". The hard common sense of the trade unions has been a safeguard against this risk, and this has been a great asset to the Labour Party. But Labour's dependence on trade union support can also be a liability if the unions are regarded by the public as pursuing narrow policies that are damaging the national economy, or if the unions use their financial power to enforce obedience to their own views.

The inclusion of marxists in the party's membership allows Conservative and Liberal opponents to remind the public of the possibility that the extremists will capture control of Labour and subordinate British interests to those of communism. The Labour Party itself has recoiled from the approaches of the Communist Party. In 1923, only three years after the British Communist Party had been founded, Labour decided that no Communist should be able to stand as a Labour candidate at a parliamentary election, and that no member of the Communist Party should be allowed to join the Labour Party. This official attitude of the Labour Party to the communists has never changed.

The anti-militarist element in the Labour Party—although Labour is not officially pacifist—has permitted critics to claim that a Labour government would neglect or muddle Britain's defences.

In general, however, Labour's problem is not so much to meet this kind of criticism, which could be dismissed as the routine of party warfare, as to adapt itself rapidly enough to changing conditions at home and abroad which play with special force on a party constituted as Labour is. The Conservatives' task is simpler: they can always apply their traditional tactic of advancing towards a new safety limit. Labour's endurance as a national party depends on the flexibility of its various parts: on the adjustments made by trade unions to suit the new place they occupy in the community; on a reassessment of the relation between private and public capital; on a new reading of the relation between the Western and communist systems; on an identification of the proper place of the individual in an increasingly centralised world; and on recognising the size and nature of the economy which Britain's position in the world can now support.

THE LIBERAL PARTY

The Liberal Party in recent years has been more assertive than either the Conservatives or Labour would have believed possible in 1945. Labour claimed to have killed the Liberal Party in 1945, if not in 1929. The Conservatives, who had swallowed first the Liberal Unionists and next the Liberal Protectionists, assumed that the Conservative Party's defence of capitalism against socialism would attract the support of all former Liberals who were more interested in private property than social welfare. Yet the Liberal Party has not only survived as an independent force but has made many gains in local government and improved its position in parliamentary by-elections.

The reason for this is the growth of a genuine concern for the protection of the individual in a society which tends more and more to be controlled either by monopoly capital or state action, or a mixture of both. Individuals are at a disadvantage in encounters with the organised power of vested interests—large industries, state enterprises, the trade unions—and the Liberals, though far more active throughout Britain than they were, have been slow to increase their tiny representation in the House of Commons—six members elected in 1959 with one by-election gain in 1962.

It may be that Liberal support will not grow to a point at which it undermines substantially the position of either of the larger parties, but the results of Liberal campaigning in the past two or three years could fairly be described as a revival, and has certainly compelled both the Conservative and Labour parties to seek reasons for them in the defects of their own policies.

The Liberal Party of to-day is virtually a new party trying to build itself up from almost nothing. The last Liberal approach to power followed the general election in 1923 when the party was united in defence of free trade against the protectionism of the Conservatives under Stanley Baldwin. In that election, 158 Liberals were returned to the House of Commons: enough to guarantee the defeat of the Conservatives and the installation in office (as prisoners of the Liberals) of the first Labour government. At successive general elections since then the Liberal representation has remained below a hundred, and even in 1929, when the Liberals ran over 500 candidates and fought on the only effective programme of economic recovery put forward by any party, "We can conquer unemployment", no more than 59 Liberals were elected to the House of Commons.

It has already been explained that Labour overtook the Liberals from 1923 onwards largely because Labour offered a real alternative to the common economic policies (apart from the free trade issue) of the Liberals and Conservatives; and so long as British politics were dominated by the experience or fear of mass unemployment, Labour held an advantage over the Liberals with millions of industrial voters. The situation changed when it appeared, after 1945, that full, or high, employment was likely to stay. But by this time, the Conservatives, influenced by such men as R. A. Butler, who controlled the party's research department, had advanced the stop lines of their own social and economic policies; and it was the Conservatives rather than the Liberals who got the benefit of a lessening of economic tension in Britain.

The slow growth of political vigour in the Liberal Party may be dated from the general election of 1950, when the Liberals ran 475 candidates and polled 2.6 million votes, compared with 13.2 million Labour votes and about 12.5 million Conservative votes. In terms of votes, the Liberals could claim, according as they were left-inclined or right-inclined, that there were either anti-Conservative or anti-socialist majorities in the electorate as a whole. This fact had a modifying influence on the attitudes of both Labour and Conservative headquarters.

But the result of the 1950 election in terms of members elected was deplorable for the Liberals; only nine Liberals reached the House of Commons, while 319 Liberal candidates had polled so small a share (less than an eighth) of the votes that they forfeited the deposit which each candidate must produce in order to stand for election. This result was not only a bitter disappointment to the Liberals, but also a profound shock. It meant in effect that the party must either die slowly of anaemia or undergo a most searching course of remedial treatment. The party preferred to seek a cure. It refused to contemplate a future in which its rôle would be no more than that of a political research group. Fortunately for the Liberals, the 1950 election had one result, not sufficiently appreciated at the time, which provided the party with a man qualified to start the work of rehabilitation: Jo Grimond, who was then aged 36, entered the House of Commons as Liberal member for Orkney and Shetland. He was a completely independent Liberal. He won the seat from the Conservatives, and against Labour opposition, with a majority of nearly 3,000 which he has increased at each successive general election. Grimond took over the leadership of the Liberal Party in November 1956 in succession to the late Clement Davies who had held this office since the general election of 1945.

Before Grimond first entered the House of Commons

he had married Laura Bonham Carter, grand-daughter of
H. H. Asquith. In a sense, this marriage gave him his
passport to Liberal politics, but his value to the party as
its leader owes nothing to this link with the party's past
fame. He was welcomed essentially as a contemporary
figure of the post-war world, and in this capacity he has
deepened the impression on the public's mind of the
modern Liberal Party as a new party, rather than as the
remnant of a body that had been lacerated in the first
world war and afterwards by feuds between the followers of Asquith and those of Lloyd George, and by
fundamental differences over protection and free trade.
The Liberal Party of to-day, while holding to its old faith
in capitalism and individual enterprise, has been willing,
as none of its rivals has been, to re-examine all its policies
to see whether they need to be adapted to fit the social
and economic conditions of modern Britain. The party's
critics object that this reformation of policy is easy
enough for the Liberals to do because they are so far
from power. But the Communist Party is even further
from power in Britain and does nothing, unless prodded
by the Soviet Union, to identify the changes that have
taken place and are taking place, and to adapt itself to
new circumstances. Moreover Liberal revisions affect the
policies of the larger parties.

Jo Grimond, as leader of the Liberals, has given
special point to two traditional elements in the party's
policy and has added a theme of his own. This he has
done on the basic assumption that the Liberal Party aims
at power, not merely influence. To Conservatives and
Labour supporters, the Liberals' struggle to regain power
has appeared either as ludicrous or impudent; but for the
Liberals themselves, and for a number of non-attached
electors, this assertion of a true political purpose has
stopped the danger of decay and despair. In 1957, when
Grimond addressed the Liberal Assembly—the policy-

making organ of the party—at Southport for the first time since he had become leader, he declared: "I am not prepared to lead a party of eunuchs. I am not prepared to lead a party which has forsworn direct political action." He gave his party ten years "to get on or get out".

The two traditional Liberal themes which Grimond has raised into prominence have been the protection and development of the individual, and the growth of international understanding. It is not difficult to make both causes meaningless by generalities, but Grimond has tried to avoid that. It would have been fatally easy to uphold the merits of individualism in terms that exposed their advocates to the charge of reverting to nineteenth century *laissez faire*, with the social evils that attended its economic advantages. Indeed, the Conservatives continually try to pin the *laissez faire* label on the Liberals. The late Lord Samuel, who at various times led the Liberals both in the House of Commons and in the House of Lords, found it necessary, shortly after 1945, to remind the public in the plainest terms that the Liberal Party had abandoned *laissez faire* long before. And Grimond's approach also avoided that trap. He spoke of the place of the individual in society when he was installed as Rector of Edinburgh University in 1961:

> If we are to maintain freedom we must have many ways in which people can participate. For freedom is partly negative. Our negative freedoms are guaranteed us by the Law and the Law Courts and they are vital. But freedom is also positive. It is the right to participate in making decisions and influencing our society. Everyone, and not merely professional politicians, must have an opportunity of making their weight felt in some organisation concerned with some aspect of running the community.

We must breed many societies, organisations, institutions, through which people can run some part of their lives. Every time the bell tolls for the take-over of a small business, every time a church closes or a local authority loses power, freedom is diminished. We should not try to stop this process, but we must ensure that it is a process of change not extinction. We must continually build up new political cells if the body politic is to survive.[10]

The Liberals have always been internationalists and supporters of the advancement of self-government of dependent territories. The party's traditional belief in the benefits of free trade assumed the existence of a world of stable, rational and friendly relations. Since 1945, the Liberals have concentrated attention on two aspects of international affairs. They tried first to promote Britain's entry into the European Economic Community well before the Conservative government decided that Britain should seek to negotiate terms of entry. (The government's efforts were thwarted early in 1963 because President de Gaulle's government in France refused to accept Britain into the Community.) Some Liberal candidates in the 1959 general election were attacked by Conservatives for advocating Britain's entry. The Liberals did not regard the case for entry solely as an economic matter. A resolution passed by the Liberal Assembly at Eastbourne in 1960 accepted the fact that the Community was "a step towards the political integration of its member nations", and urged the British government to take the lead "in establishing common political institutions for Western Europe, of which she is a part". The more extreme free traders in the Liberal Party regarded the Community as a snare: a customs union which would hinder rather than encourage the growth of world trade; but the bulk of the party were stimulated by the thought of the political advantages which might follow Britain's membership: the creation, as they hoped, of a stable, prosperous, and outward-looking regional organisation which would represent an advance towards the establishment of a world order which Liberals so ardently desire to see.

The second distinctive application by the Liberals of their internationalism was their decision to propose that Britain, while remaining a member of the North Atlantic Treaty Organisation and of the Western alliance, should abandon her independent nuclear deterrent as being economically wasteful, and as increasing the risk of nuclear war by encouraging other countries also to become independent nuclear powers. (The Labour Party later adopted this Liberal line.) The case for the abandonment of Britain's independent deterrent raises at once the question of Britain's economic and military position in the modern world which must be examined in more detail later. The Conservatives, in insisting that Britain should remain an independent nuclear power, appealed to national pride which can prove to be a strong political force; but the Liberals, over decades, have tended to follow their reason even when this has led them to adopt policies that evoked strong emotional resistance.

Grimond's peculiarly personal contribution to his party's appeal has been a challenge to the disillusioned to abandon their detachment from party politics, an attempt to bring back into the fight liberal-minded men and women who are repelled both by the Conservative and Labour Parties but hesitate to support a minority party, such as the Liberals. He appealed specially to university audiences to recognise that politics are an exciting and honourable activity, and that cynicism can be driven out of politics if individuals will make the effort to do so.

Attention has been fixed on Jo Grimond's contribution to the Liberal Party simply to bring recent tendencies into focus; but, as leader, he inherited a body which had been kept together since 1945 by the faithful service of many hundreds of people, with no hope of the temporal rewards which the larger parties could bestow from time to time, but determined to assert individual values. The organisation of capital in larger units, the growing power of the trade unions with their traditional fear of nonconformity among their ranks, the mounting cost of military and social administration which gave greater power to the central government, and the complexity of international commitments which lessened the freedom of action of the citizen: all these factors combined to alert the individual to the growing threat to his liberty; and the Liberal Party was waiting to claim and use his support.

This is not to say that the individual, or the Liberal Party, have an easy future, but it does explain the nature of the revived interest in the Liberalism which has been a feature of recent years in British politics. In parliamentary terms, the Liberals have made only a very modest advance so far. They have gained seats in local government, and this has been a benefit because it has improved the organisation on which parliamentary elections are fought. In 1958, Mark Bonham Carter won Torrington from the Conservatives in a parliamentary by-election but he lost the seat at the general election in the following year. In 1962 Eric Lubbock won Orpington from the Conservatives in a parliamentary by-election and converted a Conservative majority of 14,760 in 1959 into a Liberal majority of 7,855. This remarkable result was due partly to the patient advance of Liberals in local government in the constituency, and partly to the fact that the small-income earners who compose the greater part of the constituency had felt themselves to be the victims of the Conservative government's financial policies: wage restraint combined with high interest rates which made house purchase expensive, if not impossible.

The Liberal Party now presents itself as a radical and capitalist alternative to the Labour (and socialist) Party. Liberals claim that their policies and the quality of their candidates entitle them to the support of electors who are eager for more rapid social change in Britain but not on Labour's terms. The Liberals propose that the individual should be given a more secure and hopeful place in society through a greater share in the control of his own employment, a more equitable and generous education system, a better articulated method of expanding national production, a stiff control of urban land values, a complete recasting and simplification of the tax system, a reform of the electoral system by which minorities would be represented in the House of Commons in proportion to the total votes given them, and the devolution of functions of government to Scotland and Wales.

Such a programme appeals most directly to those who are not "organisation men", to those whose interests lie primarily outside the large power groups of capital or labour, people of small or modest income who are more interested in the contribution which they themselves can make to society (and in the services which society can provide for them as individuals) than in the collective action of the groups to which they might add power by their membership.

This manifestation of individualism is, as has already been explained, far removed from stark *laissez faire*; but the fact remains that the Liberal Party of to-day is without the backing of any powerful economic, social or religious interest. In terms of modern politics this has great disadvantages. The Liberal Party has lost the mercantile interest which, throughout the greater part of the nineteenth century, enabled the party to stand as champion of a growing but under-privileged section of the community against the entrenched power of the Conservative landowners. The capitalist element in the mercantile interest has gone over to the Conservatives; the workers' interest has gone into the trade unions and to Labour. Modern Liberalism claims that industrial conditions have improved so radically that the workers themselves will recognise more and more the invalidity of the capital versus labour dichotomy, on which the trade unions were founded, and will seek political expression through support of a Liberal Party which stresses the community of interest between capital and labour, provided that the workers have a larger say in control.

The Liberal Party has also lost the support of militant Nonconformity which gave it great vigour and moral fervour for half a century from 1870. The part played by Methodism in the growth of the Labour Party has already been mentioned, but the Liberals were the first to gain impetus from Nonconformity when, with the spread of education and the growth of industry, it was determined to assert its claim for equal treatment with members of the Church of England. That battle is over. The wealthier Nonconformists have a common interest with other capitalists in limiting the application of socialism and they tend to regard the Conservative Party as their bulwark. Social differences based on membership of the Church of England or one of Nonconformist bodies scarcely exist to-day. Archdeacon Grantley, the type of the arrogant and wealthy nineteenth century Anglican, now lives only in the pages of Anthony Trollope. The social importance in Britain of formal Christianity began to decline about the period of the first world war, which was to so many people a shattering revelation of the frailty of human nature; and it was precisely in this period that the old Liberal Party began also to decay.

THE BRITISH COMMUNIST PARTY

Karl Marx and Friedrich Engels who together published the *Communist Manifesto* in 1848 collected much of the material on which their political thinking was based in England. The remains of Karl Marx lie buried in Highgate cemetery in North London. His memorial is a place of pilgrimage for Communists from all over the world. It stands, a massive bronze bust, opposite the discreet tomb of Herbert Spencer, a political philosopher of a very different cast of mind who was contemporary with Marx. Spencer was of Nonconformist stock and was far better known than Marx to Victorian England, but it may be doubted whether one in a hundred of those who visit Marx's memorial to-day recognise the name on the tombstone opposite. For marxism, though it has not conquered England, has conquered half the world; and this is what lends importance to the British Communist Party.

This party is an outpost of Soviet communism, a branch office which distributes the opinions and acts on the orders of headquarters in Moscow—except occasionally when headquarters change their policy so rapidly that the branch office may be out of line for a day or two. To say this is in no sense to underrate the power of world communism, or to question the conviction and dedication with which British Communists act, or to deny the influence which communism has had on socialist and trade union movements in Britain. But in terms of British politics, the British Communist Party is much weaker than the Conservative, Labour or Liberal parties: it is not even autonomous within world communism. It cannot alter Moscow's policies. It is not concerned to forward British interests as distinct from Russian interests, and it is ignored by the Soviet government in official negotiations with Britain.

The British Communist Party's impact on Parliament can be described briefly. Between 1920, when the party was founded, and the general election of 1950, four

Communists were elected to the House of Commons. Since 1950 none has sat there; but in 1963 a Communist who inherited a peerage took his seat in the House of Lords and made his maiden speech—the first communist speech ever to be made in that chamber—on July 4.

The record of the Communists in the House of Commons is this. In 1922, S. Saklatvala, a Parsee, who was a member of the Communist Party, was elected as Labour member for Battersea North in a straight fight with a Conservative. No non-communist Labour candidate took part in that election. Saklatvala held the seat in another straight fight with a Conservative in 1924, but during that year the Labour Party disaffiliated Communists from its membership. As a result, a Labour candidate opposed Saklatvala at the general election of 1929 and won the seat. The figures are revealing. In 1924, Saklatvala had polled 15,096 votes against the Conservative total of 14,554. In 1929 the result was: Labour, 13,265; Conservative, 10,883; Communist, 6,554; and Liberal, 4,513. Saklatvala never re-entered Parliament.

A second Communist, J. T. Walton Newbold, was elected to the House of Commons in 1922 for the Motherwell division of Lanark. He sat in Parliament only for one year, and in 1924 resigned from the Communist Party. Newbold was one of those socialists who seek an ideal political home: he had in his time been a Fabian, a member of the Independent Labour Party, a Communist, and a member of the Labour Party from which he resigned in 1931.

The most effective Communist ever to have sat in the House of Commons was Willie Gallacher, who represented West Fife from 1935 to 1950, when he was defeated. Gallacher in his prime was a fiery but witty Scot, and he became so familiar and respected an advocate of communism in the House of Commons that his departure was regretted by members of other parties.

For Gallacher had the sense to use his opportunities in Parliament—and they were many—to fight for his cause. He no more approved of the composition of the House of Commons than any other Communist, but he was a skilled parliamentarian and never doubted that, although he could never win a vote in the House, his opponents would be influenced by the challenge with which a constant statement of the communist case confronted them. Other extremists have been too contemptuous of the parliamentary audience to try to influence it. But Gallacher was wiser: it is wholesome to have to listen to, and to answer, the worst that can be said of one's actions and policies. In 1945, Gallacher was joined in the House of Commons by another Communist, Philip Piratin, who won from Labour the Mile End division of Stepney in the East End of London. Piratin had a majority of 1,214 in a fight which a Conservative also contested. The constituency of Mile End, which has now disappeared, was one of the smallest in the country with an electorate of 16,132. By contrast, the constituency of Flint in 1945 had an electorate of 93,286. Piratin was not re-elected for any seat in 1950.

The general election of 1950 marked a stage in the attempt by the Communist Party to secure larger representation in the House of Commons. The party ran 100 candidates. Never before had it run more than 26 (1931) and never since has it run as many as 20. The 1950 effort was a total failure; and contests of special significance to the Communist Party since then have not been fruitful. In June 1963, for example, the Communists contested the by-election in South Leeds caused by the death of Hugh Gaitskell, a man whom they had condemned bitterly and consistently when he had been leader of the Labour Party for his "reactionary" policies. South-East Leeds is an industrial constituency which might have seemed to offer the Communists a better recruiting ground than some other constituencies. And the Communists had the memory of Gaitskell to challenge. Their candidate was bottom of the poll with 670 votes, compared with 18,785 for Labour, 5,996 for the Conservative and 4,399 for the Liberal. That is to say, in mid-1963, in a proletarian area of the industrial North of England, the anti-communists outvoted the Communists by 29,180 to 670.

It is an irony of the British social structure that the operation of the hereditary principle, as a means of renewing the membership of the House of Lords, should have produced the first Communist to speak in the House of Lords: the second Baron Milford, who, as Wogan Philipps, had tried unsuccessfully to enter the House of Commons in that ill-fated general election of 1950 as Communist candidate for Cirencester and Tewkesbury. Lord Milford has been given a conventional upper-class education at Eton and Magdalen College, Oxford, but the conventions of Eton cultivate an inquiring spirit and produce from time to time some unconventional politicians. Lord Milford told the House of Lords on July 4, 1963, that he would never support any measure which helped in any way to perpetuate a hereditary chamber which, he said, made no pretence to represent the interests of the British people. In his view it represented a more formidable concentration of wealth than the House of Commons had ever done since the working people had been given the vote. Britain, added Lord Milford, was the only industrial country in which the hereditary principle of choosing legislators still survived, a principle belonging to the age of the divine right of kings and entirely out of place in an age of automation, space flights, sweeping technological change, socialism, the democratic rights of the common people and the national liberation of colonial people. (All the contemporary themes which Lord Milford mentioned have been advocated in the House of Lords by various members of various parties from time to time. The House includes men who are eminent in aviation and engineering, for example.)

The Communist Party's failure in Parliament has stimulated it to seek to influence or control other organisations, and notably the trade unions. The party's power in these activities has depended on two elements: the idealism of those who seek a world brotherhood through the establishment of workers' governments, and the intellectual discipline of Communist Party members. The Russian revolution of 1917 and the establishment of the Union of Soviet Socialist Republics were watched with sympathy by many British workers, who not only shared with many other Britons a dislike of the Tsarist régime but were eager to see the foundation of a new and beneficent state run by working people like themselves, the creation of a society in which the frustrations caused by poverty and lack of education would fall away and in which a man's true ability would be fully used for the benefit of the community. Between the two world wars there were many in Britain who doubted whether such a society could ever emerge from the British parliamentary system as it was then composed.

The development of Soviet communism has proved at times to be less beneficent than the idealists expected, but even to-day the plain evidence of the power which the Soviet government has generated through a system of priorities drastically enforced, and upon the basis of a massive educational advance, excites admiration for the Russian experiment. Thus a sympathetic audience for the Communists exists, and the Communists use it through their own self-discipline. They know exactly what they seek. They know exactly how they intend to reach their goal. They master the rules of the unions, or other bodies, through which they choose to work. They attend branch meetings and stand for office. They are efficient and assiduous in performing their official duties but try to use their power to forward the aims of communism. Such activities have provoked strong resistance from anti-communist trade union leaders, who regard communism as a threat both to their own power and to the authority of the trade union and Labour movements. The late Mr Arthur Deakin, who was general secretary of the powerful Transport and General Workers' Union, was constantly on the alert to stop communist advances among union members.

The Communists' principal advance in the industrial field was to gain control of the Electrical Trades Union but that has now been broken. In 1963, they made gains in the management of the London Co-operative Society, but the Co-operative movement as a whole, which has long tantalised the Communists, retains its traditional character of a placid, workaday British institution from which millions of shoppers expect no more than value for their money and a dividend on their purchases.

The British Communist Party has failed to make a greater impact for two main reasons: first, the persistence, from a pre-1920 period, of other political means for the realisation of popular demands—not only the Labour Party but also flexible or radical capitalist parties; and secondly, the course of action followed by the Soviet government which showed that the Communists used power-politics as ruthlessly as any of their capitalist rivals.

While Soviet policies have alienated some support from the Communist Party in Britain, the influence of marxism on Labour policy is permanent. In 1948, the Labour Party celebrated the centenary of the issue of the *Communist Manifesto* by reprinting it with an introduction written by Professor Harold Laski. In this book the Labour Party stated that its roots lay in the history of

Britain but acknowledged its debts to the authors of the Manifesto. Labour policies which derived from it include the abolition of private property in land; the redistribution of the national wealth in favour of the poorer members of the community through a progressive system of taxation; and nationalisation of basic industries and services.

At the same time, Laski explained why communism as applied by Lenin and Stalin had failed to find universal support among socialists. Broadly, the reason was Russian insistence on the doctrine that outside the Communist Party no one could claim to be a socialist unless he accepted the line which at any given time the leaders of the Russian Communist Party held to be correct. This doctrine caused confusion. Communists, for example, had opposed the growth of nazism in Germany by all means in their power, but the Soviet government signed a pact with nazi Germany on August 23, 1939, a few days before Britain and France went to war with the nazis. Communist neutrality at the beginning of that war was hard for some members of the party to maintain or explain; and they had to abandon this neutrality when the nazis invaded Russia in June 1941.

Another period of confusion for communist sympathisers followed the suppression by the Russians of the nationalist rising in Hungary in November 1957. These and other incidents, including the communist blockade of West Berlin in 1948, the communist suppression of workers' risings in East Berlin and East Germany in 1953, and the building of a wall to seal off West Berlin in August 1961, had the effect of lessening the hold of communism on some of its supporters in Britain. The hard core of the party was not shaken in its loyalty; it continued faithfully to support the decisions of the Soviet government however these might veer. This loyalty, which enables British Communists to share in the strength of Soviet Communism, may be strained by the rival appeal of Chinese communism; it certainly prevents the British communists from recognising the reality of the political forces in Britain. The Communists seem not to understand the strength in Britain of the nonconformist spirit: the antithesis of communist discipline. The British Communist Party has no regard for British interests if they conflict in any way with the Soviet government's interpretation of Russian interests. Thus, the support which British Communists have given to various "peace" movements and to the Campaign for Nuclear Disarmament has never meant a communist commitment to absolute pacifism. The Communists have supported the case for the unilateral nuclear disarmament of Britain but have never proposed it for the Soviet Union. The Soviet government is quite as determined as any other power never to be at a military disadvantage. This position is well understood and, naturally, is not contested by the British Communists, who have therefore placed themselves in an equivocal position with the British public by preaching weakness in Britain while supporting strength in Russia.

PART TWO

ACTIONS AND REACTIONS

V

MONEY

1. THE AMERICAN LOAN

The Parliament of 1945, with the political apparatus
and party motives which have been described, set out to
explore the post-war world. There was immense public
curiosity about the ability of the new Labour government
to carry out its plans. People queued for admission to
the public galleries in the House of Commons. The work
and nature of Parliament was being made better known
through the activities of the Hansard Society which had
been founded by Sir Stephen King-Hall in 1944 to develop
the efforts of an earlier group he had formed in 1940, the
Friends of Hansard, to spread the fame and uphold the
standards of Parliament. For the nation, 1945 was a
moment of pride. Britain and her allies had won the war
during which, for a period, Britain had been the heart of
the resistance to nazi Germany. For Labour, 1945 was a
moment of keen expectancy. Now at last the party had
been given the power to apply the policies which it had
so long advocated and in which it believed so fervently.

The Conservatives were bewildered and embittered
by their defeat, but not for long; they soon decided to
overhaul all their policies: a task which occupied them
until 1950. The Liberals were subdued. The bulk of the
electors had preferred Labour as the party most likely to

replace the Conservatives in office. Although the Liberals were eager to support many of the reforms which Labour had promised to introduce, the party disagreed about some of Labour's plans, notably the proposal to nationalise the iron and steel industry: a disagreement which ultimately led to yet another exodus from the Liberal ranks.

Explorers expect to encounter hazards but cannot know in advance their nature or their location. So it was with the Parliament of 1945 and with successive Parliaments. The snags that were met must be described in some detail in order to explain why the political parties in Britain have reached their present positions, and what route they are likely to choose next. But the events following after 1945 will be better understood if a quick survey is made of the whole course. Britain is learning that she can maintain—and, still more, increase—the standard of living of her people only if world trade expands, and that this expansion depends on agreements made with other nations, and particularly with the United States of America.

Britain is therefore compelled to work for freer trade over the widest possible area, but she is now in a very different position from that which she occupied for half a century following the repeal of the Corn Laws in 1846. Britain's industrial revolution was then giving her the power to dominate overseas markets, and she could virtually make her own terms. To-day, she can only claim a share in world markets by accepting terms negotiated with other countries. The rôle of the United States of America has been decisive for Britain since 1945. The United States was by far the richest member of the Western alliance when the war ended, and her industrial capacity had not been damaged or destroyed during the war but greatly increased. No other state in the world was so well equipped to build up quickly the shattered economies of other countries, if it so wished. Certainly, the communist bloc was not; and Britain, whose economy had been locked in with that of the United States during the war, had no alternative but to continue the association, on whatever terms could be arranged, unless the British people had preferred on political grounds to separate themselves from the American sphere, to cultivate Commonwealth trade (if the other members of the Commonwealth agreed), or deliberately to lower their standard of life for an indefinite period by entering the communist sphere—on Russia's terms.

Most members of the House of Commons in 1945 would have recoiled from lowering Britain's standard of life any more than was absolutely unavoidable. Labour had indeed been returned to power to raise the standards of the mass of the people. Thus Britain was driven into accepting financial and trade policies promoted by the United States as a condition of securing the dollar credits which were essential, as the ministers and experts who were responsible for Britain's finances believed. This decision to enter more firmly into the American sphere has made sharp impacts on Conservative, Labour and Liberal policies. It undermined the case for imperial preference which had long been advocated by a section of the Conservative Party. It ran counter to Lord Beaverbrook's policy of empire free trade. It virtually prevented Labour from following a "socialist" foreign policy for which the left wing clamoured. It offered the Liberals a greater measure of free trade, but under stiff international controls which could only be altered or removed by agreement among the states which operated them.

The first unmistakable indication that Britain's postwar recovery would necessarily mean acceptance of stringent terms imposed from outside came with her desperate need for credit in 1945. The steps she had then to take settled her post-war course. Some individuals in all parties understood the implications of this but they were not generally realised at the time and have not, perhaps, been fully recognised yet. This lack of understanding sprang from three factors. Labour's supporters in 1945 were more concerned with the use to which foreign credits might be put than with the conditions on which they could be obtained. Many Conservatives still hoped that expanding Commonwealth trade would provide Britain's economy with the stimulus it needed. The third factor was the nature of the political battle in Britain. The Conservatives chose to attack Labour not for seeking foreign credits but for squandering the money provided. For these three reasons the public was almost totally unaware of the urgency of Britain's need to secure credits from North America—from Canada as well as from the United States—and of its consequences.

The financial events of the last five months of 1945, after Labour had taken office, were hidden partly by official secrecy and party by the victory celebrations, demobilisation and the exciting promises of Labour's programme. The new Chancellor of the Exchequer, Dr Hugh (later Lord) Dalton published in 1962 a candid account of these events.[1] In August 1945, the Treasury's view was that Britain faced total economic ruin. It had to be avoided at almost any cost. These two statements define the basis of Britain's post-war financial and economic policies. The harsh facts of August 1945 could not easily have been placed before the country, but Dalton could not hide them from his colleagues in the new government. None of his colleagues liked them and some were most reluctant to accept the consequences for their own departmental enthusiasms. It was not only the Labour government which shielded the public from the icy truth. The Conservatives had little to say about the cost to Britain of the second world war, beyond calling for the repayment of sterling credits which Britain had provided for other countries.

All the same, Britain had already learned the cost of world wars. The intensity of the economic crisis which injured so many countries in 1931 had been increased by the persistence of war debts among the allies of the first world war. The United States was the principal creditor. In 1918, the Allied powers owed the United States some $10 thousand million, of which $4 thousand million were owed by Britain. She herself was owed $7 thousand million. Most of the debt to Britain had been incurred by the Tsarist government of Russia which had disappeared by 1918. Britain could not afford to service and repay her debt to the United States. Three instalments were repaid, but the National government of 1931 suspended repayments and they were never resumed. The economic consequences of war debts were therefore familiar to the British Treasury in 1945 and even more familiar to the United States. President Calvin Coolidge, who was in office from 1923 to 1929, justified the terms on which Britain had agreed, at the end of 1922, to discharge her debt to the United States (3½ per cent interest and annual repayments of £35 million for 62 years) with the remark: "They hired the money, didn't they?" This statement, as Churchill was to observe later, was "true but not exhaustive".

In 1945, the British government was overspending its income by some £2,100 million a year. This had been made possible during the war by help from overseas, principally Lend-Lease from the United States, mutual aid from Canada, credits from the sterling area and from some South American countries. War debts had not been accumulating on the 1918 pattern because of the form in which United States aid had been given to Britain, but the fact was that Britain had been fighting and living on credit. Post-war reconstruction would have to be financed from resources which Britain did not herself any longer possess. The horror of the possibility of failure to fill this financial gap hung over those responsible for government in Britain in 1945 and can scarcely be exaggerated. Britain's shortage of resources had emerged early in the second world war. By 1940 the government was running out of funds. It was calculated that even if Britain paid out all her gold, and sold all her remaining foreign assets, she could not pay for half of the supplies she had already ordered—and these supplies were themselves quite inadequate to sustain a long war. The note on post-war reconstruction, already quoted,* which Churchill circulated in January 1943, showed already how much capital would be needed for investment at home and abroad when the fighting had stopped.

The critical financial situation of 1940 was ended when the United States Congress passed the Lend-Lease Bill in March 1941. The effect of this decision was to secure Britain's financial ability to continue in the war. No one knew at the time whether the United States would enter the war. The Japanese attack on Pearl Harbour, which brought the United States into the war, did not take place until December 7, 1941. Lend-Lease was a device adopted by President Roosevelt to permit Britain and other allies to obtain supplies without paying for them and thus without incurring a crippling debt. Theoretically Britain was hiring goods which remained the property of the United States. As the war went on, Lend-Lease was extended to the Soviet Union and to China. President Roosevelt died on April 12, 1945, and was succeeded by President Truman. The fighting in Europe stopped on May 8, 1945, and at once some members of Truman's administration proposed that Lend-Lease should stop on the ground that it had been strictly a war-time facility. On May 8, President Truman signed

* See pp. 44-5.

a document he had barely glanced at and found he had embargoed further Lend-Lease supplies. Ships which were on their way to Russia and other European destinations were ordered back. The result was consternation in the receiving countries, and the order was rescinded—but only for a few weeks.

Atomic bombs were dropped on Hiroshima (August 6) and on Nagasaki (August 9), and on August 14 Japan surrendered. Seven days later Lend-Lease had ended for good (except for China), but in December the Truman administration made a generous settlement of outstanding Lend-Lease commitments into which Britain had entered.

Before Lend-Lease had finally stopped, the Treasury's advisers in Britain, led by J. M. Keynes, raised the need for Britain to secure large credits from overseas without which, they believed, Britain's economic future would be precarious. On the day of Japan's surrender, Dalton had circulated to the cabinet an analysis of Britain's needs which had been prepared by Keynes. On August 17—four days before Truman ended Lend-Lease—Dalton proposed to the cabinet that Britain should seek, with no more delay than a week or two, to open talks in Washington on the amount and terms of an American credit. Even so, the suddenness with which Lend-Lease was stopped was a shock to the British government.

The Washington talks opened on September 11 with Keynes at the head of the British officials. At the same time the Chancellor of the Exchequer warned his cabinet colleagues that it was urgently necessary for Britain to increase and speed her exports, to convert industry from war production to commercial production, to get men back to work from the forces, to cut out inessential imports, and to reduce overseas expenditure as fast as possible. Life in Britain would be more austere (bombing apart) than at any time during the war. Dalton had difficulty in persuading all his colleagues that the situation was as bad as he believed it to be and that austerities were imperative. The general mood of the country was one of exhilaration: the war over, victory won, and a new government pledged to make a social revolution and with enough power to do so. Not even to-day, after all that has been said and written about 1945, has the nature of Britain's financial crisis in 1945 become part of the popular story of Britain's war effort. The name of Field Marshal Viscount Montgomery of Alamein still glows as a symbol of victory: Keynes and Dalton, who taxed their strength in the critical struggle for Britain's credit, have no such memorial. It is deeply sobering in retrospect to realise how little the public cared to discover about the financial events of 1945.

When the Washington talks had been first proposed, the British government estimated that, granted the most favourable circumstances, the British economy might be in balance by 1949, but that to cover the unavoidable deficits of 1946, 1947 and 1948 Britain would have to raise $5 thousand million from the United States. (The rate of exchange at that time was about four dollars to the pound.) The Treasury hoped that the British negotiators would be able to secure a free gift of $6 thousand million, without interest and without commercial conditions. The agreement took nearly three months to reach. It was signed on December 6, 1945, and its terms were stiffer than the British had originally expected. The Americans undertook to provide a credit of $4,400 million (of which $650 million represented the Lend-Lease settlement), carrying interest at 2 per cent and to be repaid in annual instalments over fifty years beginning in 1951. Britain was entitled to waive the repayment of interest, but not of principal, whenever she was short of foreign exchange. The agreement prevented

Britain from using any of this credit to reduce her debt to the sterling area, and provided that Britain should adhere to the Bretton Woods agreement. The Canadian government opened a credit of $1,500 million for Britain on similar terms.

Bretton Woods is a most important element in the story. In July 1944, the representatives of forty-four nations—an embryonic United Nations—had met at Bretton Woods, New Hampshire, to devise international bodies that would reduce the risk of post-war economic and financial collapse. The history of Germany after 1918 makes a terrifying chapter in the economic text books. It was proposed that an International Monetary Fund and an International Bank for Reconstruction and Development (known generally as the "World Bank") should be organised to start work in December 1945. Membership of both bodies carried international obligations and thus reduced the freedom of action of sovereign states. The Americans were set on removing as many restrictions as they could from the movement of world trade and on returning as soon as possible to the pre-war convertibility of national currencies, particularly sterling. Their wish was to see any holder of sterling once more in a position to be able to offer it in exchange for any other currency. The United States aimed to secure the removal of all forms of discrimination against American exports. From the British point of view, convertibility could only be tolerated if sterling were strong.

In the Washington negotiations for a financial agreement the Americans had originally proposed that sterling should be made convertible twelve months after the effective date on which the agreement began to be applied. The British did not believe that sterling would be strong enough by then to make convertibility safe. They noted that the Bretton Woods agreement proposed a five-year period of transition to convertibility. To this the Americans replied that the five-year period took no account of the provision of any credits. A compromise, painful to the British, was finally reached.

The financial agreement was approved by Parliament in December 1945. Truman signed the legislation authorising the American credit to Britain on July 15, 1946. Sterling was made convertible on July 15, 1947. This experiment in freedom, insisted upon by the Americans, lasted little over a month. The British government suspended convertibility on August 20, 1947. Suspension was felt by Hugh Dalton at the time to be a personal humiliation. He explained to the United States Secretary of the Treasury, John Snyder, that the full and free convertibility of sterling was still the indispensable long-term objective of British policy, and that suspension was to be seen purely as an emergency measure.

Later, however, Dalton saw that suspension, in the conditions of 1947, had been inescapable. In the second quarter of 1947, the drain on Britain's gold and dollar reserves had been at a rate of about $75 million a week. In July (when convertibility was authorised) the rate averaged $115 million a week. The August average was $150 million a week, and this average included the figures for the week leading to the suspension of convertibility when Britain lost $237 million. The American credit was almost finished. Dalton estimated in March 1947 that by the following February, or by June 1948 at latest, there would be nothing left to draw. But for the intervention of George Marshall, who was then United States Secretary of State, in a speech at Harvard on June 5, 1947, the prospect for Britain would have been irremediably sombre. The effects of Marshall's speech must be considered later. For the moment, the point to be made is that in 1947 Britain's economy was in a dangerous state, and that this condition was to continue. Convertibility may be taken as a test of financial and economic strength. Britain dared not make a great advance in this direction, although it took tentative steps forward, until December 1958; seven years after the Conservatives returned to office. In 1958, the Chancellor of the Exchequer, Heathcoat Amory, later Lord Amory, announced that from December 29 sterling held or acquired by non-residents of the sterling area would be freely transferable throughout the world. Repayments of the American credit may be taken as another test. Repayment of principal and interest had to start in 1951, the year in which the Conservatives returned to office. Since then, Britain has twice (1956 and 1957) exercised the right to waive repayment of interest and in 1957 repayment of principal had to be waived as well. The Conservatives were in office on both occasions.

2. THE EFFECTS OF THE LOAN

The financial events of 1945-47 set the pattern within which all British governments, Labour and Conservative, since the war have had to arrange their financial and commercial policies. The American loan will not have been fully repaid until the year 2001, assuming that international relations retain their present form, more or less, throughout that period. The political parties in Britain have had to live with the fact of Britain's deep involvement with the interests of the United States, and, broadly speaking, this fact has been accepted, tacitly or explicitly, by the bulk of the Conservative, Labour and Liberal parties. It has not been easy, however, for all Conservatives and Socialists to take the lead from the Americans. Dislike of American dominance has been revealed intermittently by minorities on both sides of the House of Commons (excluding the Liberals) since 1945. On the Conservative side, this attitude is partly a relic of the bitterness caused by the loss of the American colonies in George III's time, just as persistent American distrust of Britain's "colonialism" dates from the same period. Socialists are restive under the American yoke because it seems to them to be so blatantly capitalist.

These trends of opinion were at once apparent when the House of Commons was asked to approve the Anglo-American financial agreement on December 13, 1945. The agreement was approved by 345 votes to 98. An analysis of these figures gives a fair indication of the differences of opinion among parties over the extent to which it was believed that Britain needed credit from the United States with accompanying commitments. Those who voted for the agreement, which the Labour government had, of course, officially commended to the House, consisted of 319 Labour members, 9 Liberals, 6 Independents, 2 Communists, and 9 Conservatives and their allies. Forty-four Labour members abstained from voting. Those who voted against the agreement consisted of 72 Conservatives and their allies, 23 Labour members and 3 Independents. Conservatives who abstained from voting numbered 118. Labour members who opposed the agreement included some who were later to become part of the nucleus of a group, known as the Bevanites, which regarded Aneurin Bevan as its leader and which challenged the official Labour leadership on the grounds that it was not socialist enough and was too subservient to American policy. Among members of this group were Michael Foot, editor of *Tribune*, which offered a platform to the Bevanites; Jennie Lee, wife of Aneurin Bevan, who was then Minister of Health and who, as a member of the government, had voted for the Anglo-American agreement; Barbara Castle and Hugh Delargy. The Bevanites made their maximum effect in 1952 at the Morecambe conference of the Labour Party when they took six out of the seven constituency party seats on the national executive of the Labour Party, and defeated Herbert

Morrison and Hugh Dalton. Although this contest was not fought on the straight issue of Anglo-American relations, the defeat of Dalton had almost a symbolic significance. He it was who had persuaded the Labour government in 1945 to accept the terms for a credit from the United States, whereas those socialists who regarded Bevan as their leader, whether he was in or out of the government, were constantly trying to find some escape from the American grip. At the Morecambe conference, for example, Bevan, speaking for Labour's national executive during a debate on employment, told the delegates that the only real guarantee for the maintenance of full employment would be an understanding between governments that were applying socialist policies.

The behaviour of the Conservative members when the vote was taken on the Anglo-American agreement was even more remarkable. If Labour's left wing was determined to demonstrate in favour of socialism, fervent Conservatives were still more determined to demonstrate in favour of the Commonwealth with Britain as its leader. The motives which operated on the Conservative critics of the agreement have not yet lost all momentum. A private meeting of Conservative members was held two days before the vote was taken, and it is believed that Churchill then advised his party to vote for the agreement. The meeting showed quite plainly that a large group of Conservative members would in no circumstances do so: the most Churchill could expect was that all might agree to take no part in the voting. It was so decided. Thus, when he spoke in the House of Commons on the night of December 13, just before the vote was taken, he reminded his party of the pledge to abstain. His inability, for all his fame, to control the Conservatives on this vital issue of Anglo-American relations has been shown in the voting figures given above: 72 Conservatives and their allies voted against the agreement and 9 voted for it.

Never again while Churchill remained leader of the Conservative Party—he retired from that post in April 1955—was he faced with so awkward a position. Family ties and experience of office had combined to make him the most distinguished exponent in Britain of the need to keep Britain's relations with the United States on a firm, sound and enduring footing. His mother was an American. His dealings with President Roosevelt during the second world war had been unusually intimate. In addition, he, more than any other member in the House in 1945, knew how carefully Britain's resources had to be managed. He knew from his experience as Chancellor of the Exchequer from 1924 to 1929 how dangerous it could be to force sterling above its true value. In 1925, he had persuaded the government that Britain should return to the gold standard, from which she had departed during the first world war. This decision contributed to the economic hardship which led to the General Strike in 1926 and had to be abandoned in 1931.

Bearing these facts in mind, Churchill told the House of Commons during the debate on the Anglo-American agreement that he would deprecate most strongly any considerable number of Conservatives voting against the agreement. Such a vote, he said, would be specially injurious to British interests in America; it would be "a weak yielding to emotions which the long interest of the state requires should be stoically restrained". This, without question, was his basic position. But, as a party leader, he had two other points to make: first, that the agreement would not fetter Britain in any way in respect to imperial preference; and secondly that the terms on which the American credit had been secured were only one instalment of the "disaster" which he had predicted would follow the advent of a Labour government. No one will ever know whether Keynes, if he had been negotiating in Washington for a Conservative government, would have been able to secure more favourable terms. Sir John Anderson, later Lord Waverley, who had been Chancellor of the Exchequer from 1943 to 1945, gave it as his opinion (December 1945) that probably no better terms could have been obtained. In any case, it was the same Keynes who had been sent out to the United States in September 1917 by the Lloyd George government, of which Churchill was then a member, to assist Lord Reading to bring some kind of order into Britain's war-time spending.

No Conservative members in 1945 quarrelled with Churchill's opinion that a Labour government was a disaster but many doubted his assurance that imperial preference would not be affected by the Anglo-American agreement. The man who drew the sharpest contrast between the disadvantages of the American link and the prospect of an expanding Commonwealth was Lord Beaverbrook, the most fervent advocate of the policy of Empire Free Trade. The issue was fought between Lord Beaverbrook and Lord Keynes when the House of Lords debated the Anglo-American agreement on December 17 and 18, 1945. Beaverbrook's position was set out formally in this motion:

That this House cannot approve the financial arrangements between H.M. Government and the Government of the United States, or the participation of H.M. Government in discussions with a view to arriving at an international agreement upon the suggestions put forward by the Government of the United States, or the proposals for setting up an international monetary fund, on the ground that these measures involve a return to the gold standard, the abolition of the sterling area, and the destruction of imperial preference, all of which would endanger the economic well-being and full employment of our people, the unity of the Empire, and conditions of stable and expanding commerce essential to the prosperity of the world.

Beaverbrook showered the House with statistics designed to show that the Commonwealth had a golden future. Keynes disputed the validity of these figures, but his most telling thrust was to describe the alternative to the American link: the building of an economic block, excluding Canada and the United States, to consist of countries to which Britain already owed more than she could pay, on the basis that they should lend Britain money which they had not got, and buy from Britain goods which she could not supply. This, Keynes said, was not a caricature. (The consequences which Lord Beaverbrook foretold have not all materialised yet: Britain has not returned to the gold standard; the sterling area has not been abolished; imperial preference, though under steady attack, has not been wholly destroyed; and full employment has been maintained for most of the British people. The unity of the Empire—or Commonwealth, as it would now be called—if it is weaker, or different, from what it seemed in 1945, has been affected by a number of events in addition to the Anglo-American financial agreement.)

In the same debate, Lord Salisbury, who was then Lord Cranborne and leader of the Conservative opposition, repeated the advice which Churchill had given to the Conservatives in the House of Commons not to vote for or against the agreement. He condemned Lord Beaverbrook's intention to oppose the agreement on the grounds that the rejection of the American loan would have harsh consequences for the British people, and would bring the House of Lords into conflict with the House of Commons in the worst possible circumstances. Conflict between the two Houses, he said, might be inevitable. (It came later over Labour's proposal to nationalise the iron and steel industry.) But there could be no greater folly than to force an issue now, and on this ground.

The Lords approved the agreement by 90 votes to 8. The Bill to give effect to the Bretton Woods agreement was carried in the House of Commons by 314 to 50, and in the House of Lords without a vote.

Lord Salisbury's caution to the Conservative peers—by far the majority of members in the House of Lords, then as now—not to challenge the new Labour government on this financial issue was a mark of his leadership while the Conservatives remained in opposition. Until the controversy over the Iron and Steel Bill (1949), Lord Salisbury's influence was used, partly as a means of protecting the House of Lords as an institution, to assist the Labour ministers in the House of Lords, who could have been outvoted on every issue, in acting as the representatives of a party which had a large majority in the House of Commons.

The history of the 1945 debates contains all the elements which have been seen at intervals since then whenever Britain has been short of money. When, for example, the Conservative Party Conference was asked at Llandudno in October 1962 to endorse the Macmillan government's decision to seek Britain's entry into the European Economic Community—a policy which the United States administration warmly supported—the alternative of Commonwealth development was offered to the Conservatives by Sir Derek Walker-Smith and others. The Conference chose Europe by an overwhelming majority; and in fact the main change in Conservative opinion since 1945 has been a weakening of the belief that there is truly a Commonwealth alternative, and a growing sense that

Britain, whether she likes it or not, is fixed in the American financial and commercial system.

Labour, on the other hand, preferred the Commonwealth to Europe at its conference at Brighton in 1962 when a majority of delegates recoiled from the European Economic Community as a mechanism for advancing capitalist interests and hindering socialist controls in Britain. Labour chose a Commonwealth which it thought likely to respond more warmly than Western Europe to the kind of economic planning advocated by Labour.

Many episodes since 1945 have reminded the British people that their margin of financial stability is slight, and can be preserved only by circumspect policies. The bank rate is one index. With one brief fluctuation, the bank rate remained at 2 per cent from 1933 until 1950. (The rate was raised temporarily to 4 per cent in 1939.) But from 1951 onwards the rate has always been above 2 per cent, reaching 5½ per cent in 1956 and a peak of 7 per cent in 1957. These were the two years in which the British government was compelled to waive the repayment of the instalments of the American loan, in consequence of the financial effects of the Anglo-French attack on Egypt in 1956.

Another sharp reminder of financial instability was the devaluation of the pound which the Chancellor of the Exchequer, then Sir Stafford Cripps, had to carry through in September 1949. A second threat of devaluation occurred in November 1956 in connection with the Suez operation, when Harold Macmillan was Chancellor of the Exchequer. This threat arose in circumstances which revived in an acute form many of the doubts which had been expressed in 1945 about Britain's entanglement with the United States. The chief lesson taught by the 1956 episode was that Britain, even with the assistance of France, could no longer pay for a major military operation to which the United States, and the international agencies in which she had so loud a voice, were opposed. Britain and France launched an attack on Egypt at Suez on October 31, 1956. Cease-fire was ordered from midnight on November 6. Earlier in the day on November 6, Macmillan had asked for help from Washington in securing a loan of $1,000 million, in part through the International Monetary Fund, to prevent a devaluation of the pound. Speculation against sterling had been increasing since August as the intensity of hostility in Franco-British relations with Egypt became more apparent. Britain's gold and dollar reserves fell by $57 million in September, by $84 million in October, and by $279 million in November. During the course of November 6, the United States made it clear that a cease-fire would be a condition of any loan. Sir Anthony Eden, later Lord Avon, who was Prime Minister at the time, has stated that Britain's grim financial position was one factor which weighed with the cabinet when it decided to order a cease-fire.

One indicator of the state of Britain's financial reserves has been followed directly by thousands of citizens in their private lives: the amount of foreign currency which the holiday-maker has been allowed to take abroad with him. For some time after the war, the amount was limited and tightly controlled. In November 1959 a great advance was made. Each individual was permitted to take abroad any amount up to £250 in any one year. The limit was later extended to £250 for any one journey.

VI

TRADE AND INDUSTRY

I. THE SITUATION IN THE UNITED KINGDOM

Successive governments since 1945 have had one main task at home: to expand the production of those goods which increase Britain's earnings overseas, and especially in North America, without causing inflation and without upsetting the balance of payments. All governments since 1945 have attempted to maintain full employment, which carries with it the possibility of a labour shortage, higher wages, expensive imports and inflation. They have therefore been compelled to seek the agreement of workers organised in trade unions to policies which would limit the extent of wage increases and thus reduce the effects of rising labour costs on export and home prices. This has proved to be a delicate social operation. While the total wages bill is large, each individual's wage packet is small compared with the income of some salary earners, investors and speculators. The worker does not readily see himself as one of the 24 million employees who together take the largest part of the national income; he is a human being who wants better housing, better medical services, better schools, better conditions of work, and who sees that other members of the community enjoy a far higher standard of living than his own.

The income figures for 1961 illustrate the distribution of the national wealth (before tax): wages, £9,190 million; salaries, £5,550 million; "self employment" (professions, farming, trade), £2,160 million; rent, dividends, profit, £2,491 million. The problem has been to make the correct social equation: how much of the income of the wealthier members of the community should be taken to finance social benefits for the rest, and what would the lower income groups regard as their fair share of the national wealth? The answers have varied according to the nature of the party in office.

The first need of Britain when the war ended, as has been explained, was to secure funds with which to buy "essential" supplies: not only raw materials for industry but, for example, tobacco from the United States. The arrangements made at Bretton Woods (and later elsewhere) have been a constant support to successive British governments, although the Treasury regards it as urgent to increase international liquidity still further. This problem was discussed in detail by Harold Macmillan when as Prime Minister he saw President Kennedy in Washington in April 1962.

The events of 1956, at the time of Suez, have already been mentioned in this book. In August 1961 the British government borrowed £535 million from the International Monetary Fund but repaid it within a year, along with a credit of £323 million borrowed from the European central banks. In his Budget speech on April 3, 1963, the Chancellor of the Exchequer, Reginald Maudling, justified the use of Britain's reserves and credit facilities for building up working capital.

It is wrong to use reserves or borrowing facilities to boost up an internal position which is unsound because costs, prices and incomes have got out of hand. But it is equally unsound to refuse to use reserves and borrowing facilities for the purposes for which they exist, namely to deal with temporary situations and prevent temporary difficulties obstructing the proper long-term development of the economy.

He explained that the United Kingdom had quick access to $1,000 million through the International Monetary Fund and had total drawing rights on the fund of nearly $2,500 million. In addition, Britain owned dollar securities whose average value was about $1,000 million, and had working arrangements with the central banks of other countries in the free world. In February and March 1963, Britain borrowed $250 million to cover short-term capital movements away from sterling. In May 1963, Maudling told the House of Commons of existing short-term credit facilities and announced an agreement between the British government and the Federal Reserve System of the United States for reciprocal "swap" facilities of $500 million. At the same time, he stated that it would take long to evolve long-term credit facilities to support international trade.

Without these credit facilities the British economy would have been in grave difficulties at several periods since 1945. Even with them the position has not been easy. In February 1963, the number of unemployed was 878,000 (3.9 per cent of the insured population), which was the highest total since 1947. The causes were partly the effects of an exceptionally severe winter, and partly the effects of changes in the industrial pattern, including technological advance. At the end of July 1963, the government announced that new measures would be taken in the autumn to stimulate the economies of Scotland and the North-East Coast, where traditional, heavy industries are declining, and new work has not quickly enough provided alternative employment. These measures were to be an addition to tax reliefs for development in areas of heavy unemployment, and to the benefits of a Board of Trade control on the siting of new plant through a system of industrial development certificates. Northern Ireland, where unemployment is most persistent, was also offered special government assistance.

In 1945 the Labour government set upon its task of building a new Britain with a vast armoury of controls which it had inherited from the war-time Coalition government. The new government regarded these controls as indispensable for the direction of the economy. The Conservatives accused Labour of exercising control for control's sake. This charge was only partly true. Labour believed that it could not establish a system of economic and social priorities without strong central direction. But, apart from this consideration, the circumstances of the time compelled the government to take exceptional measures to limit consumption. In 1946, for example, a world shortage of cereals forced the government to introduce bread rationing which had been avoided throughout the second world war even when supplies from overseas were most seriously threatened by U-boat attacks. To charge the Labour government with wanting to ration bread would be ridiculous: no government in its senses would choose so unpopular a course. Bread was rationed from July 1946 until July 1948. Potatoes were rationed from November 1947 until April 1948. The Conservatives taunted Labour with the claim that bread and potatoes had never been rationed before in British history: they forgot the Irish famines of the nineteenth century which involved the British government.

While Labour had to deal with scarcity over which it had had no control, it was determined to ensure that food, building supplies, furniture and furnishings, for which there was an enormous demand immediately after the war, should be distributed according to the plan which Labour believed to be socially most desirable, on the principle of "fair shares for all". Building supplies were to be concentrated on housing, the repair of bomb-damaged property, and on schools and factories. No one was to be allowed to spend more than a fixed amount on the decoration or alteration of his property. Furniture and furnishings were rationed by dockets. Food was rationed by coupons, with a large staff of civil servants to run the food offices: a curious social institution of the time where rich and poor met each other and observed the civil service at work at close quarters. The cost of food to the consumer was kept below its economic price by subsidy. This policy was based on two assumptions: first, that it would keep the cost of living steady, discourage wage demands, and thus lessen the risk of inflation; and secondly, that a skilful government could, without damage to the economy, distribute the national income internally in any way it chose. There proved to be limits to both assumptions.

Food subsidies were, to some extent, tied to a system of rationing. Subsidy without rationing may lead to a limitless liability on the Exchequer, as the Conservative government proclaimed, after ten years of office, when it studied the ascent of agricultural subsidies. Food subsidies were introduced in 1941 during the war and they cost £63 million in the first year. In 1945-46 the cost had risen to £265 million and by 1949 to £485 million. In April 1949, the Chancellor of the Exchequer, then Sir Stafford Cripps, decided to peg the subsidies at £465 million. He reduced the limit to £410 million in the following year, and his successor, Hugh Gaitskell, retained that limit in 1951. The Conservatives have claimed that, while Labour was in power between 1945 and 1951, food prices rose by more than half.

During the general election campaign of 1951, R. A. Butler, who became Chancellor of the Exchequer when the Conservatives returned to office, gave a pledge that food subsidies would not be cut. In fact, he cut them in his first Budget (1952). He aimed to reduce them during the next twelve months from £410 million to £250 million a year, but the rate of agricultural support defeated him: at the end of 1952-53 the subsidy bill had been reduced only to £334 million.

The subsidy reductions made in 1952 were accompanied by increases in old age pensions, sickness and unemployment benefit, family allowances and tax allowances. The easing of the taxpayer at the expense of the consumer in the first Conservative post-war Budget was the start of a process of readjusting the distribution of the national income in favour of the taxpayers—those with the larger incomes—which Conservative chancellors since Butler's time have carried further. In 1957, when the government was urging restraint upon wage earners, Peter Thorneycroft extended the earned income allowance from income tax payers to surtax payers (the wealthiest members of the community). In 1961, which was another period of austerity, Selwyn Lloyd made his bold stroke of exempting incomes of less than £5,000 from surtax. When Labour left office in 1951, surtax began at £2,000 a year.

Today, subsidies are concentrated on home agriculture, milk and school meals. The Conservatives themselves were unable to abolish food rationing altogether until July 4, 1954—the British housewife's "Independence Day", as they claimed—two and a half years after they had returned to office.

A great deal of the party battle since the war has centred on the payment of state subsidies. Labour has favoured the use of them for various social and economic purposes. The Conservatives have asserted their basic disapproval of them while admitting that some subsidies must be provided. The public does not seem to have been deeply involved in the quarrel. There has been no general outcry against the regular payment of heavy annual subsidies to agriculture since the Labour government passed its Agricultural Act in 1947 which gave the home farmer guaranteed prices. A Conservative Act of 1957 broadly continued the system, which the Conservatives pledged themselves not radically to alter in the lifetime of the parliament elected in 1959. The effect of this support for agriculture has been to raise the subsidy from £321.3 million in 1962-63 to an estimated total of £364 million in 1963-64.

Three reasons for applying this system of support have been accepted as valid by Labour and Conservative governments: 1. subsidised home production saves Britain precious foreign exchange; 2. a healthy home agriculture is a social asset; 3. the system of awarding subsidies through an annual farm price review, and by means of grants for special purposes which can be varied from time to time, gives the government powerful control over the commodities produced. A shift in the subsidy can reduce the pig population, for instance, almost overnight.

Labour's Minister of Agriculture in 1947, Tom Williams, later Lord Williams of Barnburgh, was regarded by farmers and farm workers as their friend, and Labour has been determined ever since not to lose this goodwill. But the Conservatives have long claimed a special relationship with the farmer; they rely on him and his family in rural constituencies to man the party organisation. The agricultural vote in Britain comes from one of the smaller industrial groups. At the end of 1962, the number employed in agriculture and fishing was 874,000, compared with 3.4 million in engineering of various kinds, 1.6 million in construction, 1.6 million in transport and communications, and 3.5 million in the distributive trades. Moreover, the number of agricultural workers is declining (from 1.2 million in 1951) as a result of mechanisation. Agricultural workers do not solidly vote Conservative: many vote Labour and some vote Liberal. Nevertheless, the Conservative Party identifies its interests with those of the landowners. The chairman of the Conservative members' 1922 Committee—the organisation of the Parliamentary Conservative Party—has for some years been Major John Morrison, who is one of the largest landowners in Britain.

The Conservative Party always avoids, so far as it can, taking any measures that might antagonise the farmers and landowners. Yet the British government is not wholly a free agent in this matter. Commonwealth food agreements limit free action. Arrangements with meat suppliers in South America limit free action. Britain's membership of the European Free Trade Association, which began to apply tariff reductions on July 1, 1960, also limits free action: in particular, special arrangements have had to be made to protect Denmark's market for bacon in Britain. If Britain had succeeded, in January 1963, in her application for membership of the European Economic Community, more limits would have been imposed on Britain's agricultural policy.

The Conservatives gave notice during 1963 that they intended to change the method of agricultural support without, they hoped, forfeiting the goodwill of the farmers. The changes proposed were designed to bring the British system more into line with that of the European Economic Community. The government had been frightened by the double open-ended system of support which provided no limit to the quantities of commodities on which guaranteed prices had to be paid, or to the amount of deficiency payment on each unit of production so long as produce from overseas could enter Britain freely, and often at prices far lower than the guarantee.

Under the new system, protection for the Exchequer was to be provided by the establishment of "standard quantities" of the goods which the market could normally be expected to carry, and the transfer of part at least of the subsidy burden from the Exchequer to the market price. This proposal illustrates once more the Conservative policy of readjusting the distribution of the national income from the lower income groups to the benefit of the taxpayer: increased market prices would yield a concealed subsidy to the producers mostly from the mass of the consumers—the lower income groups.

The Labour government's efforts to benefit wage earners with social investment and food subsidies were only part of its plan to build a new and stable economy. Labour believed that the nationalisation of the basic industries and services would not only make the economy more efficient but give the workers a new status in society. (It would also give the government much greater economic power: a power which Conservative governments have used to deflate or reflate the economy.)

The political parties have wasted much energy since 1945 in quarrelling about nationalisation; the fact is that some post-war nationalisation was the essential condition on which the British economy could be got going again. Hundreds of thousands of working people had persuaded themselves that no economic system would be tolerable unless nationalisation were applied, and it is reasonable to assume that there would have been far more industrial unrest after the war than appeared if nationalisation had not been applied. The Conservatives, since their return to office, have never officially attempted to undo the greater part of the work of nationalisation accomplished by Labour. Gas, electricity, coal, the railways, telecommunications, the two air corporations (BOAC and BEA), and the Bank of England, remain nationalised. The Conservatives have sold back most of the nationalised iron and steel industry to private ownership, and have abandoned Labour's rather sketchy plans for an integrated transport system. But, in their handling of transport, the Conservatives found that part of the nationalised system —British Road Services—had become accepted by the users as an improvement on what had existed previously, and these services have remained part of the nation's property. The ownership of the iron and steel industry has been the chief feature of the quarrel over nationalisation. Conservatives and Liberals insist that no case has been made out for the transfer of this industry to the state; Labour, which has pledged itself to renationalise the industry, asserts that it dare not leave so much economic power in private hands.

Since so large a section of the economy is nationalised and will remain so, it would be more profitable to the nation if henceforth the political parties abandoned their tedious and irrelevant quarrel, and instead competed with each other in suggesting improvements in the economy, perhaps by state enterprise in control, management or competition, or perhaps by changing the terms in which private industry operates by new checks on monopoly practices, and by planning expansion to meet more exactly the social and economic needs of the country.

The Labour government, in its nationalisation programme, had constantly to bear in mind the wishes of the trade unions, some of which were more deeply committed to nationalisation than others. Labour had to retain the support of the unions, and wished to do so. This was not only because the unions found most of the money to finance the Labour Party, but also because, in the period of post-war shortages, with the risk of inflation, it was essential for the government to be able to count on the sympathy of the unions in any restrictive measures which had to be applied.

While Sir Stafford Cripps was Chancellor of the Exchequer (1947-50), the pressures on sterling which compelled him to devalue the pound compelled him also to impose a period of restraint on all personal incomes. He could not have attempted to restrain wages alone: to have done so would have secured a rough answer from the trade unions. On the whole, relations between the Labour government and the unions remained steady. The highest number of working days lost by strikes (official and unofficial) between 1945 and 1952 was 2.4 million in 1947. Since 1952 annual totals have reached 8.4 million (1957), 5.8 million (1962), 5.2 million (1959) and over 3 million in each of the years 1955, 1958, 1960 and 1961.

Government relations with the unions have not been altogether easy. The unions know their own power. From 1939 onwards the Trades Union Congress has been treated by successive governments as a body to be kept fully informed of industrial policy, to be consulted, and to be assured of ready access to ministers. The conditions of full employment after the war put new power into the unions' hands. With industry clamouring for labour, the unions could have held up the economy to ransom. They did not; but they had to protect the standards of their members while the cost of living was rising. Retail prices, taking those which prevailed in June 1947 as 100, had risen to 130 by the end of 1951, and have risen higher since.

The Labour government, and Conservative governments since then, have struggled with the problem of presenting economic facts in such a way that a trade union, or a group of unions, might volunteer to defer a wage claim in the national interest. To put the issue as bluntly as this is to invite the retort that no union could be expected to defer a claim which it considered justifiable, and that it is inconceivable that all trade unions would voluntarily act together to defer claims for a period. The Treasury's answer is that the total effect of a wage claim, although it may mean only a few shillings a week more in a man's pay packet, may of itself send up prices (and thus destroy the real benefit of the increase) or may achieve the same result by stimulating other claims. The Labour government attempted to create the most favourable conditions for trade union co-operation in wage restraint by imposing restraint of all incomes, and by a system of high taxation to finance social benefits. But even Cripps, who acquired unusual moral authority within his party, was unable to maintain a period of restraint for long.

The trade unions were founded to secure better pay and conditions for their members against the resistance of capitalist employers. But what happens when the employer is the state—the people, including the trade unionists themselves? This was another problem which nationalisation threw up. Industries and services controlled by the state have not yet been organised in a way which has realised the dreams of the most ardent nationalisers. Not all workers feel a personal pride in "their" industry. This is partly because the systems of management that have been set up seem too impersonal, and partly because some of the nationalised industries, and particularly the railways, have been declining. It is difficult to take pride in an industry which is bound to shrink because of economic change. In this respect, the history of British Railways has been exceptionally depressing for its staff. In March 1963, Dr Beeching, whom the Conservative government had brought into the British Transport Commission from private industry two years earlier, produced a plan for a railway system which he believed would at last pay its way, but on a scale of operation far smaller than that of the existing system.

Nationalisation has certainly brought some benefits to the workers and to the economy. The coal miners would have tolerated nothing less than nationalisation after the war, and an expensive process of modernisation and re-equipment has been carried though in the pits. The National Coal Board has established better staff relations than ever existed before in the mining industry. The chairman of the Coal Board, Lord Robens, a former Labour minister, announced in 1962 that mining had at last made a profit after a long series of losses.

A nationalised industry cannot isolate itself from economic changes, and the coal industry has found itself in sharp competition with gas (including methane imported from North Africa), oil and nuclear power. The Conservative Party supports competition and sees no reason in principle why a nationalised industry should be protected. This attitude led the government at first to propose that coal should take its chance with other fuels. This line provoked some Labour members into adopting the position that coal, Britain's most valuable raw material, should be given preference, whether or not it was the most economical or convenient fuel for the users. Ultimately the government conceded a measure of support to the coal industry, which has long been one of the staple employments in areas now suffering from persistent unemployment. As a result, a number of projected electricity generating stations were switched from nuclear-powered to coal-powered heating systems.

The closeness of the link between the trade unions and the Labour Party has kept the Conservative and Liberal parties on the alert for any signs of abuse of trade union power. Both parties accept the need to establish good relations with the unions and both claim to have assisted the growth of the unions in the past. The Conservative Party has cultivated support for Conservatism among trade union members, but the rank and file of the party showed from time to time their fear of union power and their detestation of unofficial strikes. These are condemned equally by union headquarters and by Labour, which thus brings political support to the official element in the industrial wing of its movement. Party differences about the unions can be focused on the issue whether or not a trade unionist should be under pressure to pay a political levy to the Labour Party. In 1927, following the General Strike, a Conservative government passed the Trades Disputes Act, which declared the general strike illegal in retrospect and also provided that members of unions should not pay a political levy to Labour except by their own deliberate decision: they had to "contract in" to the payment of the levy. One of the first purposes of the new Labour government in 1945 was to repeal the 1927 Act and to restore the principle that members of unions should pay a levy to the Labour Party unless they deliberately took action to contract out of the obligation. The assumption was that the political inertness of many trade union members would benefit Labour's funds. Contracting out has remained the law ever since, but the Conservatives and Liberals have meanwhile developed trade union sections; and there can be no doubt that in recent general elections very many trade unionists have voted Conservative.

To the Liberals, as chief advocates of individualism, trade unionism in its modern practice presents special problems. The "closed shop"—employment in which the unions insist that all employees must be members of a union—offends the principle of freedom of action. The Liberals do not oppose employment in which all the workers, of their own free will, are members of a trade union, and the party, like the Conservative Party, encourages workers to belong to a union. But the Liberals have been disturbed by occasional incidents in which trade union employees have refused to accept as a fellow-worker an individual who has objected on conscientious grounds to conform to trade union practices. Managements, realising that union action can dislocate their works, tend to support, or at least not to obstruct, trade unionists who seek to penalise a nonconformist. Such cases are infrequent, and the unions' demand for conformity is based on bitter experience of "break away" unions in the past which were regarded as having threatened general standards by seeking special arrangements for themselves. It has not been easy for the unions to use their power with subtlety and humanity; nor indeed have employers in the past always shown these qualities.

The need to secure the assent of a majority of the nation to awkward economic policies which faced Labour immediately after the war has faced Conservative governments since 1951. The results of the general elections of 1951, 1955 and 1959 show that the Conservatives have been successful in meeting this need, but they have done so by a refinement of the traditional demands of their own rank and file. In the general election of 1950, when Labour's power was waning, Labour had a majority of 17 over the Conservative members in the House of Commons. In 1951, the Conservatives had a majority of 26 over Labour. They increased this to 67 in 1955 and to 107 in 1959. No party in British political history had ever before increased its majority at three successive elections. There are several reasons for this remarkable situation. Contrary to the forecasts of Labour, the Conservatives have not substantially altered the social structure which Labour erected from 1945 to 1951. Expenditure on education in Britain, which cost £381.3 million in 1951-52, was expected to cost £1,118.6 million in 1962-63. This total included the cost of school meals and milk, of university grants, and of the contribution of local education authorities.

The Conservatives have shifted the emphasis which Labour had placed on the development of the social services without reducing investment in these services. Housing and the national health service—the two fields which Aneurin Bevan had to plough when he was Minister of Health (1945-51)—have been particularly affected by this shift of emphasis. The rate of house building, municipal and private, was raised by the Conservatives from 200,000 a year, the figure achieved by Labour, to 300,000 a year, but the Conservatives have increased, within this total, the proportion of houses built privately for sale and reduced the proportion built publicly for letting. The Conservatives have redistributed housing subsidies in favour of slum clearance, and have made it plain to local authorities that subsidised municipal rents should be used for the benefit of those who cannot afford economic rents, and not to assist those who can afford them. The Conservatives, who uphold within limits the virtues of a free market, passed a Rent Act in 1957 which exempted certain categories of houses from rent control and enabled landlords to benefit from free market values, and to receive a rent which was an inducement to them to maintain their houses in a decent state. Decontrol had some less happy effects. It permitted some landlords to exploit recklessly the acute shortage of housing. The remedy lay in building still more houses, not only to remove a shortage but also to satisfy an increasing demand for still higher standards of housing. House building was hampered both by the operation of a free market in land, which became very costly in congested urban areas, and by the government's use of a high bank rate to maintain the value of sterling. Dear money made municipal housing a heavy burden on the ratepayers.

The national health service, in which Labour took special pride, and which brought great benefits to the small and middle income groups, has not been weakened by the Conservatives. Alice Bacon, member of Parliament for South-East Leeds and a member of the national executive of the Labour Party, spoke of the health service in October 1962, when she addressed the Labour Party Conference at Brighton on behalf of the national executive. The Conservatives, she said, had "eroded" the health service. Miss Bacon was continuing a long Labour campaign of criticism against the Conservatives' management of this service. Labour had condemned the imposition of charges for prescriptions, spectacles and dental treatment as a severe penalty upon the chronic sick and the old. Charges, which had not been part of Bevan's original scheme, had first been authorised by the Labour government of 1950-51 as a means of restraining national expenditure in a period of financial difficulty. This decision was bitterly contested by the left wing of the Labour Party at the time, and Labour has since pledged itself to abolish the charges. But the imposition of charges has not reduced the total cost of the health service. The main change which the Conservatives made was to increase capital investment in new hospitals. A hospital plan, published by the Conservative government at the beginning of 1962, proposed to invest £570 million in hospital improvements in the following ten years.

The national health service has come to stay, although in recent years there has been an expansion of insurance schemes to cover the payment of fees for private medical treatment. The Conservatives themselves, in their own party pamphlets, boast of the success of the health service. They have reprinted a tribute paid to it in January 1963 by a social historian from the United States, Professor Almont Lindsey, who, after eight years' study of the service, pronounced it to be one of the most notable achievements of the century. It has in fact removed from millions of people the dread that they might not be able to afford the treatment which they needed; nothing now worries a British visitor to the United States more than the fear that he may fall ill while he is there and be unable to meet the cost of treatment in that country.

Labour in opposition has been exasperated by the taunt that Conservative governments have spent far more on the social services than Labour ever did—and without the use of rigid controls. The Conservatives were lucky to reach office when they did, for by 1951 the worst of the post-war shortages were beginning to end. Harold Wilson, who had been President of the Board of Trade from 1947 to 1951, had himself ordered a "bonfire of controls" before he resigned his office in April 1951, in company with Aneurin Bevan and John Freeman, as a protest against the financial policies which the Labour government was then pursuing. Marshall Aid, of which more is written later in this chapter, had worked an economic miracle in Western Europe. There had been some easement of international tension in 1954 when Sir Anthony Eden was Foreign Secretary; and in the same year R. A. Butler, who was then Chancellor of the Exchequer, told the Conservative Party Conference at Blackpool to "invest in success", and held out the prospect that Britain could double her standard of living in twenty-five years. Shortly after becoming Prime Minister, Macmillan told an audience in Bradford, Yorkshire— famous for its hard-headed audiences—that the British "had never had it so good" (July 20, 1957), and many electors were willing to give the Conservatives the credit for this state of affairs. They were helped to do so by Labour's advertisement of its internal feuds throughout the decade following the electoral defeat of 1951. Macmillan's prosperity gospel, which he was repeating as late as July 1963, was accompanied by a warning of the conditions on which prosperity could be maintained; but this was given less attention by the public and the press.

Yet it became increasingly apparent to the Conservative government that a state of economic bliss could not be maintained without ever stronger central guidance, if not statutory controls. The most striking feature of Conservative policy since 1951 has been its steady approach to central planning at home, and to membership of international economic groups abroad. Overseas commitments are described later in this chapter. In home affairs the Conservatives insisted that their idea of planning differed totally from that of the Labour Party. Labour, they claimed, would plan through physical controls and through an extension of public ownership. Harold Wilson said as much in the House of Commons on November 7, 1961. The Conservatives intended not to interfere with private enterprise but to encourage industry to be more efficient, and to acquire much more detailed information on which to base more accurate forecasts of the probable trends of trade.

In July 1961, when Britain was suffering from another bout of financial hardship, and the government had imposed a "pay pause", the Chancellor of the Exchequer, then Selwyn Lloyd, outlined a plan for a National Economic Development Council (NEDC) which, he hoped, would enable management and labour "to influence policy, to tackle in co-operation with the government the obstacles to sound growth, and to consider with us the availability and use or misuse of our resources". Those were the words in which Lloyd commended the proposed council to the Trades Union Congress when he asked it, in January 1962, to join in the work of the council. On January 24, 1962, George Woodcock, the general secretary of the Trades Union Congress, replied that the unions were "ready to give the NEDC a trial and attempt to make it work", provided that this response was not taken to imply the acquiescence of the Trades Union Congress in the government's wage restraint policy which was then still in force. Five days later Lloyd announced that the pay pause would end on March 31, and on February 2 the government published its views on the factors which should govern increases in incomes in a White Paper, *Incomes Policy—The Next Step*.

The establishment of the NEDC with the co-operation of the Trades Union Congress could well prove to be one of the decisive events in Britain's post-war economic history, even though individual trade unions approached the new order with suspicion. The conference of the Trades Union Congress at Brighton in September 1963 carried, by a majority of 6.8 million votes, a report of the general council in favour of economic development and planning; but carried also, by a majority of 380,000, a motion opposing any form of wage restraint. Supporters of this motion explained that it was intended to relate primarily to wage restraint under a Conservative government, but the decision of the conference left open the question of trade union activity under a Labour government.[1]

The membership of the NEDC included the Chancellor of the Exchequer, the President of the Board of Trade, and the Minister of Labour; George Woodcock and Frank Cousins, general secretary of the powerful Transport and General Workers' Union; and representatives of nationalised and private industry. The director-general of the council's staff was Sir Robert Shone, with degrees in engineering from Liverpool University and in economics from Chicago University, and with experience of private industry, the civil service, and a government agency (the Iron and Steel Board). In October 1962 the council announced that it was examining the implications of achieving an annual rate of growth in the gross national product of 4 per cent. Their provisional assumptions were that this would involve annual increases, up to 1966, of 5.7 per cent in exports, 4.5 per cent in imports, 3.2 per cent in consumers' expenditure, 3.6 per cent in public expenditure and 6.2 per cent in investment.

Economic development, the government insisted, must be accompanied by an incomes policy. In July 1962, during a debate on economic affairs in the House of Commons, Reginald Maudling, who had just been appointed Chancellor of the Exchequer, stated that the purpose of an incomes policy was not to keep incomes down but to ensure that they rose only as fast as the national economy could bear. The Prime Minister, Harold Macmillan, announced in the same debate that the government had decided to set up a National Incomes Commission (NIC). This commission had a less promising start than the NEDC. The trade unions refused to have anything to do with it because they did not recognise it as a body with proper authority to comment on wage claims and awards.

The commission's terms of reference were published on November 5, 1962. Maudling stated that too often in the past expansion had led to too-rapid rises in personal incomes, and that this had produced another bout of wage restraint. The duty of the commission was to examine and report publicly on wage and salary claims and awards of special national importance both in the public and private sectors of the economy. The commission had to take account of considerations which went wider than the interests of the income earners affected, such as the need to match higher incomes with higher production, and the effects of any particular wage increase on other groups of income earners. The commission was given no executive power and was not to take the place of existing mechanisms for wage negotiations and arbitration. Trade union suspicions of the new body grew when it made its first report—on a pay award to building operatives in Scotland. The commission held that this award would increase costs without a comparable increase in output. But in July 1963 the commission caused a mild sensation by reporting that another of its inquiries had been hindered by the failure of employers in the electrical contracting and other industries to provide adequate figures of the profits they had earned. This comment was welcomed by Maudling, who issued a statement upon it in which he expressed the hope that employers would give all proper aid to the commission. (It had been a constant complaint of Labour and the trade unions that Conservative governments in periods of financial stringency sought only to restrain wages, never profits and dividends.)

One other feature of the industrial field must be mentioned: the tendency of the trade unions to equip themselves more thoroughly for action in changing economic conditions. The Trades Union Congress itself has had for some time a research department whose services have been available to member bodies of the Congress. At the conference of the Congress in September 1962, George Woodcock announced that a study was to be made of the purpose and structure of the Trades Union Congress. In August 1963, the National Union of General and Municipal Workers, the third largest union in Britain, announced a reorganisation which included the expansion of its own research department. Hitherto, trade unions in Britain have been far less sophisticated than those of the United States, and have given their leaders and officials far less power and pay than are enjoyed by their American counterparts.

2. OVERSEAS TRADE

Aneurin Bevan, who shared the caution with which Labour's left wing examined United States policy, told a Labour audience in May 1948 that unemployment in Britain would have risen at once to 1,500,000 if Marshall Aid had not been available. Bevan was at that time a member of the Labour government which had jumped at George Marshall's offer of help when it had been proposed in the previous June. The conversion of Marshall's proposal into policy was accelerated by the eagerness with which the British Foreign Secretary, Ernest Bevin (who had had an outstanding record as a trade union leader), organised European acceptance of the proposal. Lord Morrison of Lambeth, who was a leading member of the Labour government of that time, wrote later that Bevin had adroitly misinterpreted as a definite proposal something that Marshall had intended to be only a feeler. It may be doubted whether any United States Secretary of State would use words in public which were capable of such a misinterpretation, but it is certain that Ernest Bevin, and those of his colleagues who knew that the Anglo-American loan was fast running out, snatched at the Marshall plan as the one means of salvation available.

Hugh Dalton, who was still Chancellor of the Exchequer when Marshall made his proposal—he resigned his office, following a Budget leakage, in November 1947 —knew better than any member of the government that new aid of some sort from the United States was the only means of maintaining and developing the British economy. Dalton's estimate of the effect of Marshall aid was that it had prevented trade, employment and living standards in Western Europe (including Britain) from collapsing quite suddenly. He ranked Marshall aid with Lend-Lease as an act of most imaginative generosity, and as a benefit to the United States as well as to Europe. It

also fixed Britain more firmly than ever in the financial
and commercial system favoured by the United States.
Upon it was based the Organisation for European Economic Co-operation (OEEC), of which Britain was a
founder member and the United States and Canada were
associate members. When the OEEC was developed into
the Organisation for Economic Co-operation and Development (OECD) in 1961, the United States and Canada
joined as full members. The OEEC was the seed-bed both
of the European Economic Community and of the European Free Trade Association.

Marshall explained his purpose in these words:

> It is logical that the United States should do what-
> ever it is able to do to assist in the return of normal
> economic health in the world without which there
> can be no political stability and no assured peace.
> The rôle of this country should consist of friendly
> aid in the drafting of a European programme so far
> as it may be practical for us to do so. The pro-
> gramme should be a joint one, agreed to by a num-
> ber of, if not all, European nations.

Marshall said it was the business of the Europeans
to draw up their own programme: the initiative should
come from Europe. It did. Marshall spoke on June 5. On
June 13, Bevin welcomed his offer in the House of Commons, and on June 27 the foreign ministers of France,
Russia and Britain met to discuss the offer. Russia rejected
it, but for a few days there was a dazzling prospect of a
break through the Iron Curtain when Czechoslovakia,
which had come under communist control in 1946,
agreed to take part in a European recovery programme.
Czechoslovakia shortly after withdrew from the project,
which went ahead without support from any communist
country. On July 12, the representatives of sixteen
nations met in Paris to prepare a statement on war

damage and on measures needed to restore the balance of trade with the United States. The plan was given to Marshall on September 22, and the OEEC was formed in 1948 to administer a European recovery programme.

The broad effect of the measures taken then, with their later developments, on the economy of Western Europe may be seen in Britain's trade figures in 1962. The value of British exports to Western Europe as a whole was 14 per cent higher than it had been in the previous year and totalled £1,359.6 million—slightly more than the value of Britain's exports to the sterling area in 1962 and greater than the total value of British exports in 1947. The value of British exports to the countries within the European Economic Community was 17 per cent higher than in the previous year and totalled £719.9 million. Exports to the countries within the European Free Trade Association, including Finland, were 7 per cent up on the previous year and totalled £517 million. British imports from Western Europe in 1962 were worth £1,378.4 million, which was slightly below the value of imports from the sterling area, but represented an increase of 3 per cent—mostly from countries within the European Economic Community—on imports in the previous year. Imports into Britain from the European Economic Community were valued at £708.5 million, and from the European Free Trade Association, including Finland, at £550.7 million.

To understand why European trade has become so important to Britain and why, therefore, Britain finds herself increasingly bound by international commercial agreements, it is helpful to work backwards from the point at which Britain's application for membership of the European Economic Community was rejected in January 1963. The British government's case for entry into the Community was made sadly plain by Duncan

Sandys, Commonwealth and Colonial Secretary, during a debate in the House of Commons on February 11, 1963, on the failure of Britain's application. In effect, he said that the negotiations had revealed "the hard economic facts" which were changing the pattern of trade between Britain and other members of the Commonwealth. He gave an impressive list of facts, including: 1. the rapid growth of British agriculture since the war; 2. the growth of industry in other Commonwealth countries; and 3. the increase in trade between Commonwealth countries and others outside: Australia's largest market for wool is now Japan; exports of beef to the United States from Australia and New Zealand are growing; Canada and Australia sell vast quantities of wheat to Communist China; and Britain's trade with Western Europe is expanding.

Inter-Commonwealth trade, in the government's judgment, offered too restricted a field for the expansion of production which should take place if the states within the Commonwealth were to raise the standard of living of their people high enough and quickly enough to make a favourable comparison with the results of communist expansion. Britain could not herself easily consume the growing volume of manufactured products from other Commonwealth countries. This was already true of the output of those areas which had been developed industrially for some time; it would become more striking as countries which had hitherto been mainly primary producers diversified their employment. And the pressure for diversification was intensified when former colonial territories acquired independence.

The problem for Britain has been illustrated vividly in the story of cotton textile exports to Britain from India, Pakistan and Hong Kong—exports which compete sharply with the output of a declining cotton textile industry in Britain. The number of men and women employed in the British textile industry declined from

1,022,000 in 1951 to 804,000 at the end of 1962. The Conservative government was unwilling to impose statutory restraint on imports from these Commonwealth countries, and preferred instead that the British textile industry should seek voluntary agreements with India, Pakistan and Hong Kong for a limit on their exports to Britain. But all these countries are in desperate need of larger markets. Hong Kong suffers from an exceptional overcrowding problem caused by immigrants from Communist China. This commercial situation has forced Labour, and some Conservative members from the cotton textile areas, into a political dilemma: are they to advocate aid for underdeveloped countries and the growth of Commonwealth trade even when the results threaten employment at home? Labour, on the whole, has preferred to fight for the interests of cotton operatives at home, but to do so has meant evading one of the awkward facts of a changing Commonwealth. This has been a curious aspect of Labour's policy, for in 1962 the party declared itself against Britain's entry into the European Economic Community, except on terms unlikely to be conceded, and held out the hope of strong possibilities for the growth of Commonwealth trade.

Britain's inability to consume the increasing production of the Commonwealth is not the only hindrance to the development of inter-Commonwealth trade. Other Commonwealth countries protect their own employment from time to time by restricting imports from Britain. In 1962, for example, Britain's exports to the United States rose by 17 per cent over the previous year's total, almost half the increase being due to the sale of cars, but exports to Canada fell by 15 per cent. This was the result partly of smaller deliveries of ships and aircraft, and partly of import duties imposed by the Canadian government.

These considerations were put before the Commonwealth Prime Ministers' Conference which was held in London in September 1962, to hear the reasons why Britain had applied to join the European Economic Community. They were in Macmillan's mind (though they were not all stated explicitly) when he addressed his party at Llandudno in October 1962. By comparison with the snags of Commonwealth trade, the developing Western European market beckoned him on. Western Europe, he said, was on its way to forming an economic and political unity which could, in terms of population, skill and resources, rival the United States and the Soviet Union. The Commonwealth Prime Ministers left Britain to decide for herself whether the terms finally negotiated were acceptable or not. They agreed to work for the expansion of world trade, for an improvement in the organisation of the world market for primary foodstuffs. They agreed that developed countries should recognise that the underdeveloped countries needed markets as much as they needed capital, and that food surpluses should be supplied to the people of countries in need. The whole emphasis of the 1962 conference was on world markets and world organisation.

The case for Britain's entry into the European Economic Community had seemed overwhelming to the Conservative government once it had reached a decision to apply for entry (July 31, 1961). But the government had been slow to find the case overwhelming. The Conservatives' search for new trade relations with Western Europe remains one of the most puzzling episodes in post-war British politics. The story starts with the formation of the OEEC in 1948. The existence of this body stimulated attempts to create new economic groupings in Western Europe. In 1952 a European Coal and Steel Community was formed by Belgium, Holland, France, Federal Germany, Italy and Luxemburg to control pro-

duction and marketing in those countries. It was successful enough to foster other groupings. Representatives of
the same six countries met at Messina, in Sicily, in June
1955 and agreed to promote a customs union. This decision led to the signature in Rome on March 25, 1957, of
two treaties by which the same six countries agreed to
form a European Atomic Energy Community and a European Economic Community, both linked with the Coal
and Steel Community. The Rome treaties came into force
on April 1, 1958.

All this activity was watched with some apprehension by the Conservative government which behaved
rather like a puppy sniffing at a hedgehog. No one knew
for sure if the European communities would work,
although the experience of the Coal and Steel Community showed fair promise. But if they did work, the
British government did not want to be totally excluded
from the benefits of the customs union. Britain was not
alone in her anxieties. All the members of the new Communities, except Federal Germany, had been foundation
members of the OEEC along with eleven other states:
Austria, Britain, Denmark, Greece, Holland, Iceland, the
Irish Republic, Norway, Portugal, Sweden and Switzerland. What were the outsiders to do?

Between the Messina conference and the signing of
the Rome treaties, the OEEC itself had surveyed the prospects for a European free trade area in which all its members might benefit. In 1956, Harold Macmillan, who was
then Chancellor of the Exchequer, had to explain to
another Conservative conference at Llandudno why the
British government was taking part in this survey. He
used some of the arguments which he repeated later in
support of Britain's entry into the European Economic
Community, but, speaking of any possible agreement, he
added: "In order to preserve the Commonwealth structure, and in view of the claims of our home agriculture,

it would be an absolute condition that agricultural products of all kinds, including manufactured feeding stuffs,
drink and tobacco, should be excluded." In February
1957, the British government placed proposals for a free
trade area before the OEEC. In March the Rome treaties
were signed. In August, Reginald Maudling, who was then
Paymaster-General, was made responsible for the British
part in the negotiations for a free trade area, and in
October he was made chairman of an OEEC committee
appointed to promote the scheme.

On November 14, 1958, the project was abandoned.
The French did not like it. The first tariff cuts within the
European Economic Community were to be made in two
months' time. When the House of Commons debated the
failure of the proposal for a free trade area Maudling
pointed out that discrimination in tariffs and quotas had
already begun to be applied by members of the European
Economic Community and that this was contrary to all
the principles of the OEEC. Negotiations, he said, should
therefore be resumed for a long-term solution which
would maintain and expand the principles and the work
of the organisation, and provide for the association of
the European Economic Community with the eleven
other members—and all this within the framework set
up by the General Agreement on Tariffs and Trade
(GATT). "We must never forget," said Maudling, "our
obligations to the free world as a whole, both in the
GATT and in the International Monetary Fund."

There followed a remarkable passage in which
Maudling scowled on the Liberal Party's suggestion—a
constant aim of Liberal policy—that Britain should join
the European Economic Community:

The consequences of this suggestion are not always
fully understood. Let us consider what would happen if we became signatories of the Treaty of Rome.

In the first place, we should have agreed to a common commercial policy, settled ultimately by a system of majority voting in which we should be in a minority. As, of our total trade, only about one-quarter is with the Six (members of the European Economic Community), it would not be easy for us to have our commercial policies with the whole world determined by agreement with our friends in the Six, who are concerned with only a fairly small proportion of our trade. That is a considerable difficulty. I must make it clear that I am referring to difficulties and not impossibilities.

Secondly, we must recognise that to sign the Treaty of Rome would mean having common external tariffs, which, in turn, would mean the end of Commonwealth free entry, and I cannot conceive that any government of this country would put forward a proposition which would involve the abandonment of Commonwealth free entry. It would be wrong of us and for the whole free world to adopt a policy of new duties on foodstuffs and raw materials, many of which come from under-developed countries, at present entering a major market duty-free.[2]

Exactly two years later (February 27, 1961), Edward Heath, Lord Privy Seal, who had been given special responsibility within the British government for European affairs in July 1960, told a meeting of the Western European Union that Britain was ready to accept in principle a common external tariff. It is not surprising that, following the lead given by Maudling in February 1959, some Conservative candidates attacked their Liberal opponents for supporting Britain's entry into the European Economic Community during the campaign which led to the general election of October 8 of the same year. Nor is it surprising that Liberal candidates who were so attacked retaliated with a bland "we told you so" when, two years later, the Conservative Party was compelled to eat its words and make a complete reversal of its earlier policy.

Labour's attitude to Western Europe since 1945 had been equivocal. The post-war Labour government did not plunge whole-heartedly into the efforts being made on the Continent to accelerate the integration of Western Europe's economy. Labour was grateful for Marshall Aid, and looked at Western Europe from inside the OEEC. An influential minority of the Labour Party, led by Roy Jenkins, accepted warmly the case for Britain's entry into the European Community, but the party as a whole preferred to stand aloof. One reason for this detachment is that elements in the Labour Party suspected that the Community would develop into an anti-communist front which would perpetuate rather than remove the division of Europe. (Mr Macmillan argued in favour of Britain's entry when he addressed the Commonwealth Prime Ministers in 1962, on the ground that Britain's representatives within the Community could act as the builders of a bridge between East and West.) Another reason for Labour's detachment was the fear that if Britain were inside the Community, a future Labour government might be stopped from applying the economic controls which it thought necessary to strengthen Britain.

The possibility of a large increase in trade with communist countries has tantalised some Labour members and a few Conservatives since the war. Trade is limited partly by the amount of foreign exchange which communist countries are willing to allot to purchases abroad, partly on the nature of the goods they are willing to buy, and partly on strategic considerations which limit the kind of goods which countries within the American system believe it to be safe to sell. In 1949, an embargo was placed by some Western countries, including Britain, on the sale of certain strategic goods to Russia, and a similar embargo was placed on trade with Communist China by a United Nations resolution of May 1951, when the Korean War was still in progress. The list of embargoed material has been revised from time to time, and occasionally British critics have alleged that other states which had undertaken to apply the embargo have been cheating. In general, British opinion has assumed that, at this stage of world affairs, no very dramatic increase in trade with the communist countries was to be expected.

The main consequence to Britain of the failure of the negotiations for a free trade area was the promotion of an alternative scheme: the European Free Trade Association (EFTA) which Labour and the Liberals have both supported. Negotiations for the formation of this body opened in Stockholm in May 1959, and by November a convention had been accepted by Austria, Britain, Denmark, Norway, Portugal, Sweden and Switzerland. The first tariff cuts for the benefit of members of the association were applied on July 1, 1960. The figures of British trade in 1962, quoted on page 160, show the relative economic strength of EFTA and the European Economic Community.

The Stockholm agreement, though better than nothing, still left unsettled Britain's relations with the Community, which began rapidly to gather strength. Between May 1959 and July 1961, when Macmillan announced that Britain would apply for membership of the Community, the Conservative government had abandoned its earlier objections to membership. Why? There were three reasons: 1. The success of the community; 2. The urgency with which the United States regarded the need to strengthen the unity of Western Europe; 3. Growing evidence of the changing needs of Commonwealth countries.

These reasons were no less valid after Britain had been kept out of the Community, and they compelled the British government to make the most of other means of increasing Britain's share of world trade. These were OECD, EFTA, and GATT. GATT had been negotiated at Geneva between April and October 1947 and came into force on January 1, 1948. It was designed as part of an international trade organisation which had been proposed in the Havana Charter, drawn up by a United Nations conference on trade and employment in Cuba at the end of 1947 and the beginning of 1948. The Charter was never ratified by the United States, and GATT is all that remains of a grand design for world trade. The purpose of the agreement is to help world trade to expand by encouraging tariff reductions through negotiations between member states, and to promote a unified system of world trade through non-discrimination. GATT has had to cover some awkward trading practices. In 1953, for example, Britain was allowed to discriminate in favour of Commonwealth goods by raising tariffs on some goods from other countries. In general, however, Britain's membership of GATT has been regarded by Conservative supporters of imperial preference as a hindrance to the growth of Commonwealth, as distinct from world, trade. Fierce battles on this issue were fought in the Conservative Party in the years following the war. The case for Britain's membership of GATT was that the agreement benefited primarily the exporting nations, and that, since Britain depended more than any other country on her exports, she stood to benefit most. In the situation created by Britain's exclusion from the European Economic Community, the British government attached special importance to the meeting of GATT arranged for the summer of 1963 to discuss proposals for a general reduction in world tariffs. These proposals became known as the "Kennedy round" because it was thought that prospects for a reduction in tariffs had been brightened by the passage of the Trade Expansion Act by the United States Congress. This Act empowered the President to cut tariffs by one half, following negotiations, and to reduce or eliminate tariffs on items of which exports from the United States and the European Economic Community together amounted to at least 80 per cent of the total exports from countries in the free world. (When this legislation was passing through Congress it had been expected that Britain was about to become a member of the Community.)

During the working of GATT there have been charges from time to time that some of its members have been guilty of unfair trading practices and have "dumped" their produce in the British market. To lessen the grievances of its supporters, the Conservative government introduced a Customs Duties (Dumping and Subsidies) Bill which was passed in 1957. Similar fears have been expressed about the development of Japanese trade which was regulated by an agreement made with the British government in 1962.

One aspect of Commonwealth trade deserves special mention. In March 1961, the Union of South Africa withdrew from the Commonwealth because South Africa's racial policy of apartheid was condemned by a majority of Commonwealth governments. This decision was announced to the British Parliament on March 16, 1961, by Harold Macmillan, who stated that the preferential trade arrangements between Britain and South Africa, governed by bilateral agreements made after the Ottawa Conference of 1932, need not be affected by South Africa's withdrawal from the Commonwealth. These trade arrangements have been maintained, but in 1963 the British government was being urged by Labour and Liberals to stop the sale of arms to South Africa, as the United Nations had recommended. The critics objected that British arms might be used to enforce the policy of apartheid (which all parties in Britain had condemned) on the Africans in the Republic. The embargo was resisted by some Conservatives on the ground that the manufacture of arms for South Africa provided precious jobs for British workers. In December 1963 the British Government gave partial support to a resolution in the Security Council of the United Nations recommending a ban on the shipment of arms and ammunition to South Africa.

This is the framework within which Britain has been conducting her international trade since the war. The effects of Britain's acceptance of international obligations on her economic position, the degree to which this has enabled her to assist the economic development of under-developed countries, and the prospects for future development will be considered in a later chapter.

VII

DEFENCE AND OVERSEAS POLICY

I. MILITARY STRENGTH

Britain found herself at the end of the war in 1945 with a share in the responsibility for the making and dropping of the first atomic bombs on Japan, and with five million men and women in the armed forces. (Britain's regular army totalled 190,000 on January 1, 1938, before conscription had been introduced; by April 1, 1964, the War Office aims at having 180,000 men in the army.) The nuclear research which led to the successful explosion of the first atomic bomb had been conducted separately in the United States and in Britain from 1939 until 1942, when British and American scientists concentrated their efforts in the United States. British consent to the dropping of a nuclear bomb on Japan had been given in principle to the United States administration on July 4, 1945, before a test explosion had proved the bomb to be an effective weapon. Within a fortnight, an atomic bomb had gone off successfully in the Mexican desert: Hiroshima was attacked on August 6, and Nagasaki three days later.

In 1945, therefore, Britain appeared to possess greater military power than she had ever controlled before. Later, she became herself a nuclear power, and she maintained conscription until the end of 1962. In

1963, for the first time since 1939, the British army consisted entirely of regulars who had joined the service voluntarily. Both the Royal Navy, whose strength should be 88,800 men in April 1964, and the Royal Air Force, whose strength should be 125,900 men, are now also on a voluntary basis. But this appearance of strength did not give successive British governments the freedom of action which accompanied great military power in the past. Britain, as has already been explained, was short of money in 1945. Her nuclear strength was then that of a partner with the United States—Congress keeping a jealous eye on American control of warheads—and the resources of the United States for weapon development were immensely greater than those of Britain. The cold war was then beginning. In 1945, the Soviet Union lacked the nuclear power of the United States and Britain, but both in manpower and in the control of resources she was a most formidable opponent. The Soviet government followed a policy which imposed on the Western powers the need to maintain forces in many parts of the world.

Moreover, the Soviet government itself exploded a nuclear weapon in 1949. The Labour government announced (September 23, 1949) that it had received evidence "that within recent weeks an atomic explosion has occurred in the USSR". It was in the same year that Attlee decided that Britain should make her own atomic bomb and be no longer dependent on shared knowledge with the United States. By 1953, the British bomb had been successfully tested in Australia. But a more powerful weapon, the thermo-nuclear bomb—the H-bomb—was already being developed, and in 1957 Britain made this too. The scale and cost of research and development were increasing. The United States and the USSR not only increased their supplies of H-bombs but developed guided missiles, with nuclear warheads, and earth satellites. The Russians were the first successfully to launch one of these satellites—"sputniks"—on October 4, 1957, and the Americans had their first success in the following year. This rivalry in missiles and satellites has proved too expensive for Britain to enter as an independent competitor. In December 1962, the British Prime Minister, Harold Macmillan, and President Kennedy of the United States agreed at Nassau that the United States would supply Britain with the Polaris missile for use in submarines, and that Britain would build her own submarines and make the nuclear warheads for the missiles. The degree of independence which this agreement left to Britain became the subject of a sharp controversy which will be considered later.

This is the general background against which Britain's armed strength must be studied in more detail. A country's military forces exist for a variety of purposes: to preserve national autonomy; to protect national interests; to extend national influence—as President de Gaulle makes plain in his policy for France; to extend national territory; to secure the continuance of a particular régime in a particular country; or to guarantee that one régime is transformed into another in conditions fixed by the controlling power. The extent to which the use of force, or the threat of its use, can secure any of these objects is limited by the availability of money, materials and men, and also by considerations of policy: what the people of a country will tolerate, what international opinion will tolerate, and what international obligations will permit. (No British government nowadays is likely to propose the extension of British territory by aggression.) An excellent example of the power of opinion to limit military action occurred in 1922 when the Lloyd George coalition government's support of Greek action against Turkey was successfully challenged. How much of her resources could Britain afford to devote to her armed strength from 1945 onwards? The Conservative Party, in its *Campaign Guide* for the general election of 1950, stated:

> Because of our need to achieve economic self-sufficiency, it is not possible for us to maintain any peace-time standing force of a size that compares with that which would be needed in the event of war. The planning of our defence forces must therefore be directed to two ends: (a) to provide regular forces within our means to carry out our policing commitments and to form a skeleton of highly trained men on which the expansion of our forces in war-time could be achieved; and (b) to train the reserves which would be needed in the event of an outbreak of hostilities.[1]

When the *Campaign Guide* was published, conscription was still in force and was to remain so for twelve more years, throughout most of which the Conservatives were in office. There were several reasons for this. The communist hold on Eastern Europe; the need to maintain the Western zones of Berlin under the four-power system set up by the United States, the Soviet Union, Britain and France; and the need to occupy Western Germany—all imposed heavy military liabilities on Britain as a partner in the Western alliance. Communist influence in the Far East, and the great stimulus to nationalism which the war had given, created many areas of instability. In 1945 Britain still held the mandate for Palestine where the Jews, determined to establish a National Home, challenged the British government and were themselves attacked by Arabs from neighbouring countries. In June 1950, troops from North Korea, which was under communist influence, invaded South Korea, which was under United States influence, and Britain answered the request of the United Nations that all its members should assist

South Korea. The fighting continued until July 1953. From 1951 to 1954, British forces were engaged in military operations against communist guerillas in Malaya. In October 1956, Anglo-French forces undertook "armed intervention" against Egypt at Suez.

Disturbed international conditions were not the only reason for the maintenance of conscription. Military forces are increasingly mechanised and must be serviced by a growing army of technicians. But in post-war Britain the imperative need to develop the economy, and the existence of full employment, offered technicians opportunities of civilian employment which many found to be more rewarding than those of military service. The armed forces would have been starved of the skilled men they needed unless military service had been made compulsory, or until service conditions had been brought closer to those of civilian life. It has taken successive British governments a long time to improve service conditions to a point at which they could compete, on a voluntary basis, with those of industry. Conscription has itself played an important part in modernising service life. On the other hand, from the professional serviceman's point of view, the conscripts were a nuisance. They had not, of their own free will, accepted the conventions of military life. They kept judging service life by the conditions they knew outside and to which they would shortly be returning. They exposed the private world of the professionals to the gaze of undedicated laymen. They complained to their MPs. But in many respects the results were wholesome. There is no reason why any country which decides that it must have armed forces should impose on its servicemen and women conditions which are markedly worse (allowing for the proper demands of military service) than those of civilians. The conscripts, in leaving the services, also left behind a barracks-building programme.

There was another compelling reason for the maintenance of conscription in 1945. Many of those who had been called up in 1939 or immediately afterwards had served six or five years in war-time and were due for release according to age and length of service under a system that had been devised to avoid the errors of demobilisation after the first world war. Men with long service had to be replaced if the release scheme were to work equitably—which was its whole point—and if essential post-war tasks, particularly those of military government in countries where normal civil conditions would take time to re-establish, were to be completed.

One of the first decisions of the Labour government in 1945 was, therefore, to continue conscription in peacetime. This was the first occasion in British history when conscription had been imposed in peace: the start of conscription in 1939, before war had been declared, had been a prelude to a conflict which seemed inevitable. Many observers in 1945 thought it a bold decision for a Labour government to take since British tradition had been opposed to conscription, and the Labour tradition had been opposed to militarism of any kind.

Although sections in the Labour and Liberal parties were opposed to conscription, the decision to maintain it aroused remarkably little resentment in general public opinion. Those who cared about the politics of defence saw for themselves that post-war conditions were confused and dangerous. The minority of the British public which preferred the communist system to that of the Western democracies could not oppose conscription on principle, for it was part of the communist defence system. But most of those liable to be conscripted almost certainly held no strong political views at all. For them, the tests were to be the nature of the military service to be performed (was it to be something purposeful, or merely "spit and polish"?), and the comparison of service pay and conditions with those of civilian life.

The Labour government provided, in the National Service Act, 1947, for the continuance of conscription until 1954. Conscription was retained by the Conservatives after that date, but in 1957 the Conservative government decided to revert to regular, volunteer forces from the beginning of 1963. The application of this plan was slightly delayed by a short-term decision to keep specialists with the forces for six months longer than their normal term of national service.

The *Statement on Defence, 1962* contained an explanation of the Conservative government's belief that Britain, almost alone in NATO, could afford to do without conscription. The government stated that Britain, if she were to discharge her world-wide responsibilities, had to be able to bring to bear, at very short notice, forces which were ready to fight. This could only be done with highly trained, well equipped formations, with great long-range mobility. In the government's view a period of conscription could not be long enough both to enable men to be adequately trained and to have them available for a worthwhile period of active service after training. (During 1962-63, for example, British troops were called on to perform special emergency duties when disturbances broke out in Brunei and British Guiana.) The British government certainly counts the nuclear deterrent as some compensation for the reduction of the services to their present size; for it has answered critics of the policy of maintaining an independent nuclear deterrent with the argument that its abandonment would involve a return to conscription.

Conscription in Britain, with special provision to permit conscientious objection, worked remarkably smoothly. The principal objection to it, apart from the dislocation which it caused in the lives of some individuals, was and remains its wastefulness. To get the servicemen required, conscription produces others who are not really needed but who still have to be trained, fed and paid with the rest. In general, the British take easily to service life; and it would be wrong to suppose, even in an age of nuclear weapons, that men and women will cease to volunteer for the armed services. In fact, the more mechanised these services become, and the more dependent they are on the unity of small groups of skilled men, the more the services are likely to appeal to those elements in the British which provided the volunteer forces of the past. The British make good soldiers, and the military record of the country is perhaps better remembered by the public than some observers at home and overseas might suppose. In public estimation, the Royal Navy can do no wrong; the Royal Air Force, in its encounter with the Luftwaffe in the Battle of Britain, strengthened the nation's pride; and the army added Alamein to Waterloo in its roll of honour.

The British have a taste for tests of endurance, and they accept hazards which they could avoid. One of the notable social developments in recent years has been the adaptation of battle-training methods, used in the second world war, to cultivate resource and endurance in conditions of physical discomfort or danger. The Outward Bound movement, and other organisations for men and women, exist to provide in peace-time such moral and physical training. The stimulus of danger is no new experience. Oliver Cromwell summoned a parliament in 1656 when conditions in Britain were still disturbed after the Civil War, and he told it of continuing threats to the existence of the Protectorate. "Well," he said, "your danger is as you have seen. And truly I am sorry it is so great. But I wish it to cause no despondency, as truly, I think, it will not: for we are Englishmen; and that is one good fact."

The peril of nuclear warfare has, naturally, greatly increased the public demand for international disarmament. The activities in Britain of the Campaign for Nuclear Disarmament and of the more militant Committee of One Hundred have constantly forced the public to face the meaning of nuclear war. At its most intense, the Campaign for Nuclear Disarmament has challenged civil authority in Britain with a persistence which has come nearer than anything else has done to that shown by the suffragettes just before the first world war when more extreme demonstrators got themselves killed for their cause. Yet neither the Conservative, Labour nor Liberal parties have officially proposed that Britain should deny herself access to nuclear arms so long as they are available to the communist world. All three parties stand for general disarmament if it can be done so as to preserve, at every stage, the balance of forces between the communist and the Western defence systems. It was on this account that the nuclear test ban agreement signed in Moscow in 1963 by representatives of the Soviet, United States and British governments, was welcomed in Britain by all parties as a step towards general and balanced disarmament. The three parties have not only refused to deny Britain whatever protection access to nuclear weapons may give, but have also committed themselves to improve Britain's conventional forces. The British Communists have been disingenuous in their attitude to nuclear arms: they have supported unilateral nuclear disarmament for Britain but would not dream of proposing it for the Soviet Union. Their Dove of Peace carries an olive branch to the East and a nuclear bomb to the West.

There has been one sharp difference of policy on nuclear arms between the Conservatives on the one hand, and Liberals and Labour on the other. Liberal policy on the deterrent, which has been described earlier, has diverged markedly from that of the Conservatives since 1957; formally embodied in a resolution carried by the Liberal Assembly at Eastbourne in 1960, it has been re-affirmed since. The Eastbourne resolution "recognises that the defence of Britain must be founded on a policy of collective security. Whilst deploring the tendency to rely increasingly on nuclear weapons at the expense of conventional forces, the Assembly reaffirms its support for NATO as a necessary shield in the West until multilateral disarmament has been achieved." The Liberals then proposed that more effective joint control should be created over the use of nuclear weapons "and of all operations on or from British territory by American forces".

The Labour Party followed the Liberals in adopting the policy that Britain, while remaining in the Western alliance, should abandon her independent deterrent. The Labour Party found herself in a curious position after it had left office in 1951. The bulk of the party did not know that the Labour government had authorised the making of a British atomic bomb until Clement Attlee's successor at Downing Street, Winston Churchill, told them so. For some years after leaving office, Labour officially approved of Britain's possession of an independent nuclear deterrent; and Hugh Gaitskell, after he had succeeded Attlee as leader of the Labour Party, argued in the House of Commons that Britain needed its own deterrent because circumstances might arise in which British and United States policies were not identical. But the Liberal decision was too much for the Labour Party which could not afford, on such an issue, to stand to the right of the Liberals. In any case, a large minority within the Parliamentary Labour Party, and an even larger proportion of delegates to the Labour Party Conference, were eager to go further than the Liberals. A resolution in favour of unilateral disarmament for Britain was carried by a small majority, against Hugh Gaitskell's impassioned resistance, at the Scarborough conference in 1960. This decision overturned Labour's traditional support of collective security which had led it to base its foreign policy on membership of the League of Nations after the first world war, and on that of the United Nations after the second world war. The Scarborough decision was reversed the following year at the Labour Party Conference at Black-pool. Gaitskell, who had pledged himself at Scarborough to fight for the rejection of unilateralism, told the Black-pool conference that Labour's national executive was opposed to the unilateral nuclear disarmament of the West because "if we were to do so, we should be exposing ourselves, all of us in the alliance, to every possible threat or pressure that a fully armed Soviet Union chose to bring to bear upon us". He declared his passionate belief that if Britain were to become neutral and were to give up the NATO alliance, "which Ernest Bevin played such a very large part in creating", it would be profoundly dangerous for the peace of the world.

Harold Macmillan's government, with the massive but not quite unanimous approval of the Conservative Party, sought to maintain Britain's independent nuclear deterrent on the grounds that the possession of such power served the national (as well as the international) interests of Britain, secured Britain a place in international discussions from which she might otherwise be excluded, and strengthened the close link between Britain and the United States which had been made when both nations co-operated to produce the first atomic bomb. (The cost of the nuclear element in Britain's armed forces has been estimated by the government to be about one-tenth of the total defence budget, which for 1963-64 stood at £1,837.7 million.)

The Macmillan government never defined the circumstances in which Britain might decide to use, or threaten to use, her own nuclear weapons independently of joint action by the Western allies. In fact, it is clear that the threat to use nuclear power would not enter at all into many policy decisions which a British government might back by a threat of military action. A hypothetical case—the defence of Britain's three Protectorates in South Africa, Bechuanaland, Swaziland and Basutoland—was brought into the public's mind in September 1963, when Dr Verwoerd, the Prime Minister of the Union of South Africa, suggested that his government should administer the Protectorates. One of them, Basutoland, is completely surrounded by Union territory, and another, Swaziland, is nearly so. There would be very strong opposition from all parties in Britain to the transfer of responsibility for the Protectorates from Britain to South Africa in present circumstances. The British government is pledged to make no change without consulting the wishes of the people of the Protectorates. But, however sharp the differences between the British and South African governments may be on racial policy, it has never been suggested by any party in Britain that a British government should if necessary be prepared to impose a policy against South Africa by threat of nuclear attack.

The Conservatives assumed that they would receive widespread national support for the retention of a British independent nuclear deterrent; and it was to secure the independence of the deterrent that Macmillan made his agreement with Kennedy at Nassau at the end of 1962. The occasion for this meeting was the decision of the United States administration to cancel plans for the production of the Skybolt missile, which was also to have been supplied to the V-bombers of the Royal Air Force. Kennedy offered to continue the development of Skybolt —a complex and expensive weapon system—if Britain would bear half the cost. The Prime Minister would not accept such a commitment for three reasons: 1. Skybolt might not be a success; 2. no one knew when it might be ready; and 3. no one knew what the final cost would be. Macmillan accepted Polaris missiles instead.

The Nassau agreement was criticised by the Labour and Liberal parties, and by individual Conservatives (but not by the party as a whole), as reducing rather than maintaining the independence of Britain's nuclear deterrent. While Britain, under the agreement, was herself to make the submarines that would carry the Polaris missiles, and the nuclear warheads for the missiles, the missiles themselves were to be bought from the United States, which might interrupt supplies either for technical, political or industrial reasons. The joint communiqué issued by the President and the Prime Minister after the Nassau conference (December 21, 1962) suggested that the President was more concerned with the nuclear strength of the Western alliance than with the independent nuclear power of Britain.

> The President and the Prime Minister agreed (stated the communiqué) that the purpose of their two governments in respect to the provision of the Polaris missiles must be the development of a multilateral NATO nuclear force in the closest consultation with other NATO allies. They will use their best endeavours to this end. . . . The Prime Minister made it clear that except where Her Majesty's Government may decide that supreme national interests were at stake, these British forces will be used for the purposes of international defence of the Western alliance in all circumstances.

The terms of the communiqué raised a doubt, which could only be tested by action, whether Britain's "supreme national interests" could ever nowadays be challenged except in conditions which threatened the

Western alliance as a whole; whether, that is to say, Britain's Polaris missiles would ever be of use except as part of the defence system of the West?

It is not necessary in a survey of this kind to describe in detail the use which Britain has made, or has not made, of her armed strength since 1945. The major events of the period have been widely reported. It should be said, however, that British governments have not been very effective when acting alone, or with a single partner, outside the domestic duties of the Commonwealth. On the other hand, the British have taken a large share in common action to maintain the position of the West in the cold war. But the possibilities even of collective action have been shown to be limited in this dangerous world. The Western powers dared not use their military strength to assist the Hungarians who asserted their nationalism against Russian control in 1957. For the West to have acted would have been to risk war with the Soviet Union; they did not court this risk, and the Soviet government was therefore able to restore its control over Hungary.

The difficulty of Britain's position can be shown in a few examples. British arms were unable to secure conditions in which the British government could make a settlement between the Arabs and Jews in Palestine while Britain held the mandate for that country. No other power, and certainly not the United States, was willing to share with Britain, after the second world war, the task of applying a policy which frustrated the Jewish plans for a National Home: an object which it had been Britain's duty to promote under the terms of the Balfour Declaration of 1917 and of the mandate given to Britain by the League of Nations in 1918—and which, at the same time, antagonised the Arabs. When the British surrendered their mandate to the United Nations and left Palestine in 1948, the State of Israel was proclaimed. The events of

1945-48 in Palestine were one of the most grievous episodes in British history, and imposed a severe strain on
British troops, who were attacked by Jews and Arabs
alike. Churchill, who was then leading the Conservatives
in opposition and who had been a constant supporter of
the Balfour Declaration, condemned the Labour government in 1949 for its lack of a Palestine policy which, he
said, had lost Britain the chance to bring perfectly legitimate pressure on the United States to "come into the
arena of useful action", and which had cost Britain £80
million for the troops alone.

A second illustration of the ineffectualness of
Britain's armed strength in a situation where she was
acting alone occurred in March 1951, when the Persian
government decided to nationalise the oil industry in
which the British government had a large interest through
its holdings in the Anglo-Iranian Oil Company. Lord Morrison of Lambeth, who was Foreign Secretary at the time,
wrote in his *Autobiography* that the Conservatives had
accused the Labour government of allowing Britain's
valuable oil installation at Abadan to be "stolen". Lord
Morrison commented that if military action were to have
been effective it should have been quick, and that he himself, as Foreign Secretary, had thought there was much to
be said for sharp and forceful action. The cabinet, he
stated, had been left in little doubt that it would take a
lot of time to mount an attacking force, which might
therefore fail. The Labour government decided that force
would only be used if it were needed to protect British
nationals. In the end, and after Labour had left office, a
consortium of oil companies, including United States
firms, was formed and made an agreement with Persia to
run until 1979, with a further option of fifteen years. It
was a condition of the agreement that the Persian government was to receive half the earnings.

The failure of the joint Anglo-French attack on

Egypt at Suez in 1956 showed the British forces hampered neither by will nor courage but by political and financial considerations. Britain, as has been explained earlier in this book, could not secure essential credits from the United States to support sterling if she continued the attack. This was a case in which Britain, even with the eager support of France, could not sustain a campaign when faced with the disapproval of international partners, not only in the United States but within the Commonwealth and the United Nations.

An example of successful British action, in co-operation with her allies, occurred in the air-lift to West Berlin which was made to overcome the blockade of that city imposed by the USSR from June 1948 to May 1949. West Berlin is surrounded by communist-controlled territory, and it was as part of the cold war that the Soviets threatened the access of the Western powers to Berlin. In twelve months from June 1948, British and American aircraft carried nearly two million tons of freight—coal, food and oil—into West Berlin. British airmen took 23.5 per cent of the total, and the cost to the British tax-payer was £8.6 million. (The cost of all overseas actions has been a recurrent theme in British politics since 1945.)

In several important instances since 1945, British forces have been used successfully in the domestic rôle of policing disturbed areas of the Commonwealth. Two instances in particular must be mentioned. From 1951 to 1954 British troops were engaged in fighting communist irregulars in Malaya. As a result of the campaign, conditions were created in which Malaya proceeded to independence: the Federation of Malaya Independence Act was passed in 1957. In 1952 and 1953, British troops also took part in a campaign in Kenya to control the activities of Mau Mau, a secret terrorist organisation wielding fearful power over the Africans. Here, too, conditions were created in which Kenya made a great advance to independence, which she acquired at the end of 1963.

2. OVERSEAS POLICY

(i) *Foreign Affairs*

British governments since the war have continued, but with a new sense of urgency, the traditional British policy of seeking allies to preserve common interests without war. The production of thermo-nuclear weapons by the two great power blocs centred on Moscow and Washington has accelerated the process of compelling nations to choose between East and West. Such security as may be found, short of balanced disarmament, is sought by many nations in membership either of the Soviet or the American defence systems. Nations which have recently become independent, particularly in the Afro-Asian group, have attempted to avoid any such commitment but this has not always proved easy. India, for example, which became independent in 1948, retained her membership of the Commonwealth without accepting any Commonwealth defence commitments. She saw herself within the Commonwealth as, so to speak, a peace-bridge between East and West. But China's attack on India in October 1962 showed how difficult it might become for any large nation to preserve a position of detachment in a restless ideological world.

Differences between China and the Soviet Union have made it easier, in this threatening situation, for India to seek military aid from Russia as well as from the West. If relations were to worsen, and Chinese pressure on India to be intensified, Russia's access to India through Afghanistan might be seen as a means of mutual aid; and then at last the link between Russia and India, which always looked so alarming to British governments in the days of the Tsarist régime, might be made.

Britain herself has never attempted to become detached from world affairs. She is firmly within the American system until a world order has been established; but the consequences of this position have led to much political controversy, both in the Conservative and Labour parties. The Conservatives, while accepting wholeheartedly a Western alliance to contain communism, are nevertheless jealous of the power of the United States. Britain's entry into international agreements and groupings since 1945 has constantly raised Conservative doubts about the strength of the control or influence which Britain's representatives may exercise. A series of meetings between British prime ministers and presidents of the United States since 1945 has obscured to some extent the strength of the uneasiness felt in some sections of British opinion on this score.

The issue was seen at its plainest between October 22 and 28, 1962, when the British government appeared to the public to have no voice whatever in the decisions which President Kennedy took to challenge the Soviet build-up of nuclear missiles in Cuba which were directed against United States territory. Harold Macmillan said of these events that the world had been brought very near the edge of nuclear war. While the Cuban crisis lasted, Macmillan announced the British government's complete support of Kennedy's action, but the fact remains that Britain's principal ally took rapid decisions, involving the risk of nuclear war, acting alone. On October 28, Khrushchev, the Soviet leader, accepted the demand of the United States that the Cuban bases should be dismantled under United Nations supervision. This result was interpreted by some nations which had been unsure of the moral strength of the Kennedy administration as clear evidence that the new President would take the sternest action in defence of Western interests.

Conservative opinion is not only jealous of American power but exasperated by the refusal of the United States at times to support or, as the Conservatives see it, even to try to understand, British policy. Two instances have already been mentioned: Palestine and Suez. In no area since 1945 have Anglo-American relations been less coherent than in the Middle East; and British opinion is always ready to suspect that the cause of the differences between the two countries in this area is to be found in the politics of oil.

Britain's membership of the American defence system has created even greater difficulties for the Labour Party: its social democracy prefers, on the whole, Western freedom to Eastern control, but its socialism is deeply suspicious of American capitalism and offended by the persistence of the colour problem in the United States. The detailed application of Western defence policy creates even sharper difficulties for the Labour Party, whose members wonder if the British government has the power to stop any trigger-happy anti-communist in Washington from adopting a reckless course. During the Korean war, Clement Attlee, who was then Prime Minister, flew to Washington to dissuade President Truman from permitting an extension of allied bombing across the Yalu river into the mainland of Communist China. In 1960, the discovery of the flight of a United States reconnaissance plane over Soviet territory, just before a Summit meeting was to be held in Paris, was received almost with horror by the Labour Party—and did not please the Conservative government, either.

Labour has, however, been most disturbed since 1945 by the problem of defining the place of Western Germany in the European defence system: can Western Germany be trusted never again to abuse her power, politically and militarily? (The Conservatives have themselves been a little uneasy about Western Germany but they have been more ready than Labour Party members to make room for Western Germany in Britain's alliances.) This question has troubled Labour not only because the record of the nazis, particularly their anti-semitism, has left an indelible mark, but also because Germany is the West's frontier in Europe with the Soviet defence system. There is some sympathy in Britain, among members of all parties, with the situation of the Poles, whose communism seems less rigid than that of any other communist state in Europe except Yugoslavia. No one who recalls the nazi attacks on Poland and on the Soviet Union, and who appreciates the military convenience of North German plain, can fail to understand Polish and Russian fears of a revival of German aggression. Thus Harold Wilson, when he visited Moscow and Warsaw in June 1963, as leader of the Labour Party, said in Moscow, and repeated it in a broadcast from Warsaw: "We, as the Labour Party, are opposed now, and in all future circumstances, to the provision of nuclear arms to Germany, or to any German finger on the nuclear trigger, direct or indirect."

This policy decision to deny Western Germany an equal share with other allies in the defence of Western Europe creates more difficulties. During the same visit to Moscow, Wilson said that Labour supported the rights of the people of West Berlin (who were then governed by the Social Democratic party) to choose their own form of government and to be assured of access to the West. But Social Democrats in Western Germany, and members of other West German parties, have found Labour's attitude to the future of their country rather confusing and a handicap in promoting the Western connection. The Labour Party's decision to invite Willy Brandt, the Governing Mayor of West Berlin and a leader of the German Social Democratic Party, to be the guest of honour at a rally to mark the opening of the Labour Party

Conference at Scarborough in September 1963, was part of an attempt to improve relations between the two parties. Labour would infinitely prefer a solution of the German problem based on some system of demilitarised zones in East and West Germany than to have to deal, in office, with a divided Germany playing an active part in both the Eastern and Western defence systems.

There is no mistaking the extent of the suspicion with which many Labour supporters, and particularly the left wing, regard the rearming of Western Germany. The Labour Party Conference at Blackpool in 1961, which reversed the unilateralist decision of the previous year, also carried a resolution condemning the Conservative government's decision to permit the training of West German troops in Britain. (Nevertheless, the troops came and were trained.) While Labour's rank and file observe Western Germany with distrust, the party officially committed itself to the rearmament of Western Germany in 1954. (The Labour government had committed itself in 1950.) The close division of opinion within the Labour movement on this issue was shown in a series of votes in 1954. On February 23, the Parliamentary Labour Party supported German rearmament by 113 to 104. On February 24, the national executive of the party supported it by 16 to 9. On September 28, the Labour Party Conference at Scarborough supported it by 3,270,000 votes to 3,022,000. The resolution which was then adopted called for self-government for the Federal German Republic; for arrangements to permit West Germany to contribute to collective security "in a way which would preclude the emergence again of a German military menace"; and for more efforts to reunify East and West Germany on the basis of free elections.

The Liberal Party has been less querulous than either of the others about Britain's rôle in post-war international obligations. In marked contrast to the attitude taken by

Labour and Conservative leaders, Liberal opinion welcomed the proposals for a European Defence Community, thwarted in 1954 by British indifference and French opposition. The party has been concerned to see that all the states which enter into military agreements should share more effectively in political control of military decisions.

The spinning of a network of regional agreements within the American and Soviet defence systems since 1945 is a sign of the failure of the members of the United Nations to agree upon a form of world order. One consequence of this failure has been the growth of minority movements within the Western system advocating federal union or world government, but progress towards both objectives has been blocked by the mutual distrust of the Western and Eastern powers. How much the governments which founded the United Nations expected of it is difficult to say. Those who had supported the League of Nations after the first world war certainly hoped that the defects of the League would be corrected in the formation of its successor. The absence of the United States from the membership of the League had proved a fearful weakness, and it seemed imperative to those responsible for planning the United Nations that terms should be arranged which would guarantee the presence within the new body of the two most powerful states in the world: the Soviet Union and the United States.

This was the origin of the agreement made at Yalta (February 1945) between Stalin, Roosevelt and Churchill. They decided that the Security Council of the United Nations, which was to hold responsibility in the new organisation for the maintenance of peace, should take no policy decision without the agreement of the council's five permanent members: the representatives of Britain, Nationalist China, France, the United States and the

Soviet Union. The representative of each of these states had, therefore, the power of veto. This indeed was the condition on which Russia's presence in the United Nations could be secured. After the United Nations had been set up (October 24, 1945), the veto was first seen to be a weapon in the cold war by which the Soviet Union prevented the Security Council from endorsing Western proposals regarded as hostile to communist interests. For some years the Western powers pilloried the Russians for their use of the veto, but, as the Security Council extended its activities to touch direct British interests, Britain's representative on the Security Council was instructed by Conservative governments (the Labour governments of 1945-51 never issued such instructions) to veto the taking of decisions.

On September 13, 1963, Britain vetoed an Afro-Asian resolution which sought to prevent Britain from transferring military and political power to the "White" government of Southern Rhodesia, and to delay the grant of independence to Southern Rhodesia. The resolution was designed as a protection of the interests of the Africans in Southern Rhodesia. In 1956, Britain, supported by France, twice vetoed the taking of decisions hostile to their joint attack on Egypt. France used the veto on two other occasions and Nationalist China used it once. So far, the United States has never used the veto. When the Security Council decided to support South Korea in resisting the attack from North Korea, the Soviet representative had been absent from the meeting. Yet, despite the use of the veto, no member of the United Nations has insisted on changes in the organisation which might lead to the withdrawal of the Soviet Union. For all its defects, the United Nations is regarded as an indispensable international meeting place: better that the Russians and the Americans should meet on neutral ground, even if they quarrel, than that they should meet nowhere. There is one dangerous omission from the membership of the United Nations—Communist China. All parties in Britain support her entry, but the United States, with its long and close ties with Nationalist China, now based in Formosa, has consistently opposed it.

Labour and Liberal foreign policy since the war has been founded on support for the United Nations as the only existing means of creating ultimately an instrument of world order. Conservative governments since 1951 have also supported the United Nations but have been critical of some of its more recent activities, and of the tendency of the growing Afro-Asian group of countries in the United Nations to urge upon Britain a more speedy transfer of power from colonial administrations to independent governments in Africa. Conservative doubts about the United Nations were voiced by the present Prime Minister, Sir Alec Douglas-Home (formerly Lord Home) when, as Foreign Secretary, he said, at Berwick-on-Tweed on December 28, 1961, that he detected a "crisis of confidence" in the United Nations and that this raised the question whether the United Nations had had its day. He accused the Afro-Asian countries of adopting a double standard of judgment: one for the Russians, whom they feared, and another for Western democracies because they reasoned and compromised. Britain, he said, was moving fast, perhaps faster than she should, in granting independence to former colonial territories, and he added: "Since we in Britain are agreed on independence anyway, the only way to pick a quarrel is over timing: self-government today, regardless of whether there is anyone capable of governing—independence tomorrow, even though it would mean other Congos."

Lord Home contented himself with a warning. The British government has never proposed that Britain should withdraw from the United Nations. But his sharp attack on aspects of the work of the United Nations expressed the views of a large body of Conservatives who resented the "interference" of the United Nations in Commonwealth policy. There has always been, on the other hand, a small core of Conservatives determined to support and develop the United Nations, and some of them have joined the Parliamentary group for world government. Labour and the Liberals dissociated themselves from Lord Home's attack.

The more the United Nations intervened in world affairs the more the loyalty of its members to the conception of world order, as distinct from the preservation of national interests, was tested. In 1948, after Britain had surrendered to the United Nations her mandate for Palestine, the Security Council appointed Count Folke Bernadotte, nephew of the King of Sweden, as mediator in Palestine. He was murdered by terrorists in Jerusalem on September 17, 1948. United Nations forces were later posted in the Gaza strip to maintain the cease-fire of December 1956, between Egypt and Israel. When civil war broke out in the Congo in 1960, United Nations forces sent there to keep the peace were involved in heavy fighting.

Activities such as these created serious political differences in Britain. Many Conservatives were made uneasy by the Congo operation, particularly as it affected the province of Katanga, with its industrial interests. But the government did not go to the extent of expressing its political disapproval of the United Nations by withholding financial support. The communist and Arab states refused to contribute to the cost of maintaining United Nations forces in the Middle East. The communist states, with France and Belgium, refused to contribute to the cost of the Congo operation. It has been estimated that up to the middle of 1963 the accumulated deficits on the Middle Eastern operation was about $27 million, and on the Congo operation about $73 million. The United

Nations organisation was faced with bankruptcy and proposed the issue of United Nations bonds as a means of relief. At the beginning of 1962 the British government decided to buy $12 million worth of these bonds. A group of Conservatives at once signed a motion in the House of Commons proposing that the representative of any member state of the United Nations which had failed to pay its contributions should not be permitted to speak or vote on any resolutions, or to move any resolution, until the deficit had been made good. (This would, of course, have shackled the Soviet representative.) This motion was countered by that of a smaller group of Conservatives who expressed their support of the United Nations by restating the actual provisions of that body. Their motion urged the government to continue its full support of the United Nations, and expressed the view that no member who was more than two years in arrears with its financial contribution to the regular budget of the United Nations should be allowed to vote in the General Assembly, "as provided by article 19 of the Charter".

After the foundation of the United Nations it soon became clear that those of its members who were being drawn into the Soviet or American power systems would seek greater security for themselves in military alliances. The Western powers became alarmed by Russia's consolidation of her hold on Eastern Europe. On March 5, 1946, Churchill delivered a speech at Westminster College, Fulton, Missouri, in the presence of President Truman, in which he advocated the formation of a "special relationship" between the British Commonwealth and Empire (as he called it) and the United States, carrying with it the continuance of the existing facilities for mutual security—a relic of the war—by the joint use of all naval and air force bases in the possession of either country all over the world. Such an alliance, he said, would not conflict with the general interest of world agreement.

The candour of the Fulton speech was a shock to many Labour members in the House of Commons, but the Labour government and its successors have followed the aim which Churchill had indicated. The "special relationship" for which he had asked was real enough fifteen years later to provoke the envy of President de Gaulle in France, who tended to regard the exclusion of France from similar intimacy with the United States as a humiliation that must be obliterated. The consequences of the French attitude became so embarrassing to the promoters of Western European unity that when Macmillan returned from his Nassau meeting with Kennedy in December 1962, he played down the notion of a special relationship between the United States and Britain.

Regional military agreements were slow to take shape after the start of the United Nations. The first object of the British government was to create a system of collective security in Western Europe, to make sure that the United States took part in it, and to discover some means of allowing Western Germany to share in the burden of Western defence without alarming the former enemies of nazi Germany.

The first agreement was made in the Brussels Treaty of March 1948, between Belgium, Britain, France, Holland and Luxemburg. They bound themselves to take such action as they deemed necessary if one of them were attacked, and to give each other all the military and other aid in their power. The signatories set up a consultative council of ministers to co-ordinate foreign policies; a permanent commission of ambassadors; and a permanent military committee. On May 5, 1955, Italy and Western Germany became members of the Brussels group, which was transformed into the Western European Union. On the same day, Western Germany became independent. The proliferation since 1945 of international organisations to which Britain has been in some way committed has left the British public slightly confused and rather bored. The man in the street is unlikely to know what the initials "WEU" stand for, yet Britain's membership of the Western European Union has involved a limitation of her sovereignty and a lessening of Parliament's authority. Some members of Parliament were shocked to discover that the Union could take defence decisions, even affecting Western Germany, without the need to secure the approval of the House of Commons. And it was to the Union's council of ministers that Edward Heath, Lord Privy Seal, gave a fuller account than he did to Parliament of the commitments which the British government might undertake if Britain entered the European Economic Community.

After the Brussels Treaty had been signed as a stop-gap in the defence of Western Europe, the North Atlantic Treaty was signed in April 1949 between the signatories of the Brussels Treaty (who did not then include Italy and Western Germany) and the United States, Canada, Denmark, Iceland, Italy, Norway and Portugal. The two North American powers became linked directly with Western Europe in the military arrangements of the North Atlantic Treaty Organisation. This has remained the basis of collective security in the West supported throughout by the Conservative, Labour and Liberal parties in Britain, but with some restlessness on Labour's left wing because NATO has been deeply concerned to prevent a defence vacuum from being created in Western Germany. Moreover, NATO became balanced in Eastern Europe by the signatories of the Warsaw Pact: the Eastern European Mutual Assistance Treaty. This treaty was signed in May 1955, five days after the Western European Union and a sovereign state of Western Germany had been created. The original members of this alliance were the Soviet Union, the German Democratic Republic (East Germany), Czechoslovakia, Albania, Bulgaria, Hungary, Poland and Rumania. Albania later ceased to be a member because she sided with communist China in that country's quarrel with the Soviet Union: a quarrel which assumed major importance in 1963.

British attitudes to the balancing forces in NATO and in the Warsaw agreement had differed, especially in the Labour Party. Labour supporters, whose first aim is to reduce tension between the West and the Soviet Union, have seen Western European Union and NATO as provocations which made the Warsaw alliance inevitable, as hindrances to better relations. Officially, however, the Labour Party has regarded this balance as a possible basis for negotiating the creation of a nuclear-free zone, or at least a zone of controlled disarmament, in Central Europe on the kind of lines suggested in February 1958 by Adam Rapacki, Foreign Minister of Poland. No agreement between East and West to try such an experiment has yet been reached.

Signatories of the North Atlantic Treaty bound themselves to regard an attack on one of them as an attack on all, and to take such action as was deemed necessary in the event of an attack. No signatory was automatically compelled to fight, and the United States congress retained the power to control the entry of the United States into war. The United States has dominated NATO because of its overwhelming strength. Latterly, other members of NATO have grown increasingly concerned to share more fully in the control of NATO's power. The United States administration itself recognised the strength of this demand. When Kennedy and Macmillan met in England in June 1963, they issued a joint statement in which they agreed that "a basic problem facing the NATO alliance was the closer association of its members with the nuclear deterrent of the alliance". They also agreed that the allies should confer on the American proposal for a multilateral sea-borne force, armed with medium-range ballistic missiles, but "without prejudice to the question of British participation in such a force". There was widespread opposition in Britain to this proposal when it was first made. Conservatives doubted whether it would be workable from a military point of view or justifiable on economic grounds. They much preferred that Britain should continue to contribute her own units to NATO, rather than that British troops should be one element in crews of mixed nationality. Labour objected that "mixed manning" might permit a German finger to release the nuclear trigger; for in 1949, Western Germany, along with Greece and Turkey, had joined NATO.

How was Western Germany's power in men and materials to be used in defence of Western Europe? North Korea's attack on South Korea in June 1950, following the Soviet blockade of West Berlin, drove the Western powers to seek a West German contribution to defence which might be acceptable to all the Western allies, and particularly to France. (Throughout the arguments over Western Germany, British governments were concerned to limit the cost in foreign exchange of maintaining British forces in Germany.) In September 1950, the United States administration warned the North Atlantic Council that unless European members of NATO decided at once in favour of the rearmament of Western Germany, the United States might withdraw from an integrated European command. In the following month, a French plan for a European Defence Community was accepted by the French National Assembly. This proposed the formation of a European army in which West German battalions would be distributed among European brigades; there was to be no German army as such.

Many months of anxious negotiation followed. In September 1951, the foreign ministers of the United States (Dean Acheson), Britain (Herbert Morrison) and France (Robert Schuman) met in Washington and declared their support for the European Defence Community, and a treaty providing for its establishment was signed on May 27, 1952, by the foreign ministers of Belgium, France, Holland, Italy, Luxemburg and Western Germany. On the previous day, new contractual agreements with Western Germany had been signed in Bonn by the allies and these ended formally the occupation of Western Germany. However, the French National Assembly rejected the EDC treaty, and Western Germany was not admitted to a close military alliance with the West until she joined Western European Union in 1955.

Western Europe was only one of the regions in which Britain sought and accepted international obligations, all limiting her own sovereignty to some extent. Agreements were also made covering areas of the Middle and Far East.

At the height of Britain's imperial powers, towards the close of the nineteenth century, she protected her interests in the Middle East and the route from India to Britain through the Suez Canal from a base in Egypt. This base was retained until the end of the second world war, but the growth of nationalism in Arab countries, the establishment of the state of Israel, and the inquisitive watch kept on that part of the world by the Soviet government, all increased the strain on the British garrison in the Suez Canal zone. The garrison became expensive to maintain and difficult to protect against a hostile Egyptian population. In 1950, Britain, France and the United States issued a tripartite declaration guaranteeing the status quo in Israel. This was intended in effect, though not in form, to discourage Arab states from threatening or attacking Israel. And there were, naturally, questions asked in the House of Commons about the validity of the tripartite declaration when Israel invaded Egypt in 1956; this was a situation that had not been foreseen six years earlier.

Britain's support for the new state of Israel, and Egypt's consistently provocative attitude towards that country, worsened Anglo-Egyptian relations and strengthened the case for Britain's withdrawal from the Suez Canal zone on the best terms that could be got. Before Labour left office in 1951, negotiations had started for a new treaty with Egypt and for the arrangement of a new relation with the Sudan which had been ruled in condominion by Britain and Egypt—in effect, by Britain —since 1899. Sudan, like Egypt, was pressing for independence, and in any case Egypt was not prepared to remain Britain's sleeping partner in the control of the Sudan. Britain reached an agreement with Egypt on the Sudan in 1953 with the result that the Sudan became fully independent at the beginning of 1956, thus ending a period of British rule which had started with the murder of General Gordon at Khartoum in 1885.

In 1954 the Conservative govenment signed a treaty with Egypt which provided for the evacuation of British troops from the Suez Canal zone by June 1956. Between 70,000 and 80,000 troops were involved. Their maintenance had cost Britain £50 million. In addition, the government owned vast military installations in the zone which had no true economic value. Egypt undertook to provide Britain with the facilities to put the base on a war footing and to operate it effectively if there were an attack on Egypt, or on any member of the Arab League (which was then composed of Egypt, Saudi-Arabia, Iraq, Jordan, Syria, the Lebanon, the Yemen, Libya and the Sudan), or on Turkey. Some Conservatives in Britain were shocked by the willingness of a Conservative government

to agree to the withdrawal of British troops from the Suez
Canal zone, a withdrawal, as they saw it, from imperial
power. The Foreign Secretary who had negotiated the
treaty with Egypt, Anthony Eden, was sharply criticised
by a group in his own party. The fact that he had had to
bear such criticism in pursuance of a policy that placated
Egypt contributed to his anger when later the Egyptian
government nationalised the Suez Canal Company (July
26, 1956) in which Britain was a large shareholder. To
Eden this seemed like paying good with evil. Egypt's "in-
gratitude" played a part in forming his decision, as Prime
Minister, to join with France in an attack on Egypt a few
months later. To compensate Britain for the loss of the
Suez base, the government developed military facilities in
Cyprus, which was then a colony. The new military importance of Cyprus was a major factor in stiffening Conservative opposition to the Greek Cypriot struggle for
union with Greece. When finally agreement was reached
in 1959 on the basis of Cyprus's independence within the
Commonwealth, the new state formally authorised
Britain's use of military facilities in the island.

In looking back on the post-war relations between
Britain and Egypt it seems evident that even if the Anglo-
French attack on Egypt in 1956 had been maintained and
had secured key-points along the Suez Canal (as the combined forces might well have done), the cost of maintaining an occupation garrison would, in terms both of men
and money, have been far higher than in the period leading to the treaty of 1954. Egypt would certainly have
intensified her attacks on the garrison and on supplies,
with the support of the roused nationalism of her Arab
allies. The evacuation of the Canal zone had been decided
upon by the government in 1954 partly because the cost
of maintaining the garrison was so expensive in foreign
exchange, and partly because the rôle of a vast, static
garrison was thought to be losing its military importance.

Mobile reserves based in Britain were to be built up instead.

There was another development in the Middle East. In 1955 Turkey and Iraq signed the Bagdad Pact for their mutual defence. Britain, Pakistan and Persia adhered to it from the start, and in 1957 the United States, without signing the Pact, started to send representatives to the economic and military committees of the Bagdad organisation. In 1958, Iraq ceased to participate, and in 1959 withdrew from the organisation which moved its headquarters to Ankara and was transformed into the Central Treaty Organisation.

The attempt to provide security in the Far East has been hazardous. The British government was offended when, in 1951, Australia, New Zealand and the United States signed the ANZUS Pact in San Francisco without asking Britain to join. The Labour government's spokesmen admitted at the time that they would have preferred Britain to be a signatory of the Pact. Conservatives condemned the government for a lack of initiative which had caused Britain to be excluded from it. The three signatories each agreed to act to meet any danger which might follow an attack in the Pacific area. The willingness of two members of the Commonwealth to enter into such a commitment with the United States meant that they recognised the dominance of the United States in the Pacific area and did not regard the Commonwealth link as offering comparable protection. Britain undertook a different Far Eastern commitment in 1954 when she signed the South East Asia Treaty at Manila. This treaty established an organisation for collective security with the support of Australia, France, New Zealand, Pakistan, the Philippines, Thailand and the United States. The treaty provided that its terms would not apply in the event of an attack either on Formosa or on Hong Kong. The organisation has no common command or military structure, but left wing opinion in Britain has regarded it with suspicion on the ground that it might become an instrument of the United States in increasing American dominance in the Far East and in checking national self-determination in Vietnam and Laos. East and West have been constantly on guard in that area, although the principal powers concerned have formally continued to apply the uneasy agreements, made at Geneva in 1954, with the intention of reducing tension.

(ii) *The Commonwealth*

Changes in the Commonwealth since 1945 have been so rapid and widespread that some of the substance underlying them has been ignored or misinterpreted. The trend of the changes has been indicated in the alterations which have been made by the government in its administration of overseas affairs. In July 1947, the Commonwealth Relations Office came into existence. It took over the functions of the Dominions Office which had been created in 1925 by Leo Amery, as a condition of his acceptance of the office of Colonial Secretary, when the Conservatives returned to power in 1924. (Amery himself filled both posts.) Leo Amery was a passionate Commonwealth-Imperialist, and in 1924 he persuaded the Prime Minister, Stanley Baldwin, that the development of the more advanced countries which owed allegiance to the British Crown would be stimulated if the government's relations with them were removed from the management of the Colonial Office to a new department, of which the very title would indicate their separate status. The word "Dominion"—British Dominion—was chosen to mark this advance. The new department governed Britain's relations with Canada, Australia, New Zealand, South Africa, Rhodesia and the Irish Free State, which had been set up in 1922. (In 1948, the Free State became the Republic of Ireland—outside the Commonwealth.)

Twenty years after the Dominions Office had been established, the word "Dominion" had become irksome to the countries which it was supposed to describe and no longer represented the relation to Britain in which they saw themselves. They were willing to act as equal partners with Britain in a "Commonwealth", but not in an "Empire", nor even in a "British" Commonwealth, and this fact was recognised by all parties in Britain, though with more reluctance in the Conservative Party than elsewhere. Thus in 1947 the Commonwealth Relations Office was formed, and six months afterwards another change was made which was the formal expression of the most radical development in Commonwealth affairs that had hitherto occurred: India and Burma became independent, and the India Office and the Burma Office, which since 1937 had been managed by one minister, were wound up. Britain's relations with India were from that time controlled by the Commonwealth Relations Office; Burma became an independent state outside the Commonwealth. One other administrative change reflecting developments in Commonwealth policy has taken place. In July 1962, Duncan Sandys, the Commonwealth Relations Secretary, became also Colonial Secretary. The balance of work between Commonwealth and Colonial affairs had been reversed since Amery had held both the Secretaryships of State in 1925. At that time, the duties of the Colonial Office were far the more onerous; but by 1962, Commonwealth affairs—that is, the relations of the British government with independent states within the Commonwealth—had overtaken colonial affairs in volume and complexity, because the advance of colonies to self-government had been so rapid. Duncan Sandys's assumption of the two offices was accompanied by another change: Britain's relations with the three Central

African countries—Southern and Northern Rhodesia and Nyasaland—which had hitherto been the responsibility partly of the Commonwealth Relations Office and partly of the Colonial Office, were put under the control of one minister, R. A. Butler, First Secretary of State.[2] A smaller administrative change must also be mentioned. In July 1961, a new Department of Technical Co-operation was created to supervise and expand Britain's assistance to overseas countries. This function had previously been divided between four departments: the Foreign Office, the Commonwealth Relations Office, the Colonial Office, and the Ministry of Labour. This development was a sign of a shift in Commonwealth policy. It was the result of a growing conviction that, although Britain must continue to provide development and welfare grants and loans to Commonwealth countries, there was an increasing demand for a different kind of help: the sharing of knowledge and technical ability, both by sending British specialists overseas and by providing more places for overseas students in Britain.

Throughout this period of change, British governments have been subjected to many pressures from the growth of nationalism, and to some criticism from countries outside the Commonwealth. The broad effect of all this has been to create in some minds the impression that Britain has been compelled, by forces which she could no longer contain, to surrender her imperial power. The notion of Britain as a crude colonialist bully has been given currency both by the Soviet government, which has a political interest in discrediting Britain, and by some elements in the United States who have inherited the emotional resistance of their forefathers of George III's time to Britain's overseas policy, or the Irish memory of Cromwell's rule and of the famines and evictions in the nineteenth century. Roosevelt himself was not free of suspicion of British colonialism. Outside opinion, however, has not always interpreted the transformation of the British Empire into a Commonwealth in terms that accurately represent the attitude of a majority of the British people to this event. The British as a whole are not ashamed of their record. It was notable that the Labour Party, in its criticism of the negotiations for Britain's entry into the European Economic Community in 1962, saw greater merit in the Commonwealth than in Western Europe.

Britain's imperial power has obviously diminished, and the transfer of power has, obviously, been accelerated by the growth of nationalist feeling which it would have been too expensive in lives and money for Britain to resist indefinitely. But the record of Britain's colonial administration and of her politics shows conclusively that there have long been formative elements in the country consciously working for the transfer of power to independent governments. No doubt British governments might have chosen, if they could have done so, to delay the transfer of power in particular countries until conditions seemed more settled, and to be satisfied that independence would guarantee completely the preservation of minority rights. Events have forced the pace. But it is remarkable that, with the exceptions of the Republic of Ireland, Burma, and the Union of South Africa, the Commonwealth has lost no members since 1945 and has gained the support of all the territories which have become independent in that period. The newer members of the Commonwealth tend to choose republican status for themselves and not to accept allegiance to the Crown as part of their membership of the Commonwealth, but there is no evidence that the polite rejection of this mystical bond has made any practical difference in the relation of members of the Commonwealth to each other.

What does "support" of the Commonwealth now

mean? Is it a matter for pride that the British Empire has become a loose association of autonomous states with varying and divergent interests? Even if the remaining ties of the Commonwealth were blown away tomorrow —gossamer in a puff of wind—the fact that they ever existed at all would remain a remarkable episode in human relations. The Commonwealth in itself threatens no one. It can do no harm, but it may promote understanding and prosperity between races of different colour and belief throughout the world who consult with each other in a completely free association. This statement of the Commonwealth's rôle may make it appear to some of small account; but it would be rash, in the restlessness of to-day, to brush aside any international association which provides means for the regular exchange of ideas intended to improve international relations, and in conditions which reduce, if they do not altogether eliminate, the rivalries which are so marked a feature of the relations of the power blocs in the United Nations.

The multi-racial Commonwealth is still so new and tender that the British may look upon it with astonishment as well as pride, but this does not weaken the strength of the feeling which binds many British families to the older members of the Commonwealth. There is a domestic link with relatives in Canada, Australia, New Zealand, South Africa and Rhodesia. There are sporting ties—the long series of test matches with Australia, for example. There is the shared experience of two world wars. No estimate of the British attitude towards the Commonwealth should undervalue the living bond between the British and their kinsmen overseas.

Since 1945 the commercial interests of the various members of the Commonwealth have become increasingly diversified, and to some extent conflicting, but British governments have been able to rely in their dealings with other members of the Commonwealth on a sympathetic and rational exchange of views. Without compulsion, British Chancellors of the Exchequer have been helped from time to time by their Commonwealth colleagues to strengthen the reserves of the sterling area. Latterly, the trend of Commonwealth inclinations— "policy" would be too stiff a word—which has emerged from periodical meetings of Commonwealth finance ministers has been to promote freer world trade as the best means of increasing the prosperity of each member of the Commonwealth.

In the busy process of constitutional change within the Commonwealth three areas demand special reference: India, South Africa and Central Africa. The India Independence Act of 1947, which changed British India into two independent states of India, dominated by the Hindus, and Pakistan, dominated by the Moslems, did more than any other event to transform the Commonwealth.

Clement Attlee, as Prime Minister, was himself responsible for fixing the timing of the transfer of power. The Labour government announced in 1946 that the British would leave India in 1948, and this statement precipitated the partition of British India in 1947 into two autonomous states. Attlee chose Lord Mountbatten of Burma to be the last British Viceroy in India, imposing on him the duty to ensure that power was in fact transferred. The separation of India and Pakistan from British control was the end of one dream and the beginning of another: the stopping of an outlet for British greed, idealism, combativeness, orderliness, sense of adventure and phlegm; and the opening of a vision of Commonwealth in which master and servant should become equal, richer and more benevolent by recognising at last each other's true worth. So much has been written about British rule in India that it is not necessary to elaborate upon a record in which magnanimity, cruelty and fantasy are all combined. The final verdict upon this period of British history was given in the readiness of independent India and the new, independent Pakistan voluntarily to maintain and develop cordial relations with Britain after 1947, and to invite British specialists of various kinds to take service under their respective governments.

The fascination which India and Pakistan have exercised over so many Britons for so long has not lessened since those countries became independent. There has been a ready acceptance of service in the new conditions. Perhaps the most vivid illustration of the strength of the link between independent India and Britain was provided during the Commonwealth tour which Harold Macmillan, as Prime Minister, undertook in 1958. He was the first British Prime Minister ever to set foot in India, and the warmth of his welcome made a deep impression upon him. For he was not only Prime Minister but leader of the Conservative Party which, in accordance with its traditional belief in the prudence of advancing cautiously, had been least eager of the British political parties to hasten the grant of independence to India. It cannot be doubted that Macmillan, with his strong historical sense, was profoundly moved by the generosity and friendliness of the Indian people. The importance, in the development of Commonwealth affairs, of the mutual respect of the Indian and British governments could scarcely be overestimated. India asserted a different political emphasis from that made by Britain. She wanted no part in military obligations undertaken by other Commonwealth countries. Although in her domestic policy India has shown moments of aggressiveness, she was pacific in her outward gestures and a constant advocate of the virtue of creating a truly multiracial Commonwealth. India's attitude to defence irritated Conservative opinion in Britain. No consequence of India's independence was felt more sharply by Conservatives than the loss of this reservoir of troops, and the closing of a period of military history in which the British army in India, and the Indian army with British officers, had played an eventful and notable part. (The old Indian Civil Service, controlled by devoted British administrators, might be said, however, to have made a more lasting mark on Britain's relations with India.) The British government agreed in 1963 to provide military assistance to India when she was attacked by Communist China. But India sought aid from other countries, too, the United States and the Soviet Union among them.

Pakistan has never wished to keep out of military arrangements. She joined the Bagdad Pact organisation when it was formed in 1955 and remained a member when it was turned into the Central Treaty Organisation. Britain, anxious to remain on intimate terms both with India and Pakistan, tried repeatedly but without success to find a way of ending the dispute between the two countries over Kashmir, which is now part of India although most of its people are Moslems.

Ceylon and Burma were granted their independence at the same time as India and Pakistan, but Burma, unlike the other three did not accept a Commonwealth link. The economic implications for Britain of the creation of four entirely independent and autonomous states, which had all formerly been strongly affected by Britain's commercial policy, are self-evident. With growing populations and an inadequate standard of living, these countries had to develop industrially and follow policies designed to strengthen their own economies, irrespective of the effects on Commonwealth trade. In fact, remarkably few clashes with Britain's commercial interests resulted from this situation. Wherever friction appeared, efforts were made to ease relations by voluntary agreement. Lancashire's cotton textile industry secured some relief by such means from the free entry into Britain of the textiles of India, Pakistan and Hong Kong. The British government also sought by voluntary agreement to reduce the flow of immigrants into Britain from India and Pakistan. Nevertheless, the future export needs of the developing countries may create new problems for Britain.

The free entry of Commonwealth goods into Britain was of mutual benefit so long as Britain could export her manufactured goods in exchange for raw materials. This balance began to be upset by the development of secondary industries in the countries that produce raw materials; and it was largely because of this that Commonwealth finance ministers started to emphasise the importance to the Commonwealth of an increase in world markets. The need to develop secondary industries was accepted as essential if the poorer countries were ever to reduce the gap, which is still widening, between the poorer and the richer countries in the Commonwealth, and if the Commonwealth itself were to counter the economic attractions of communism. Representatives of the Commonwealth governments agreed at Colombo in 1950 on a plan to assist this economic process in South and South-East Asia. The beneficiaries were India, Pakistan, Ceylon, Burma, Nepal, Thailand, Vietnam, Laos, Cambodia, the Philippines, Malaya, Singapore, Indonesia and Borneo.

The withdrawal of the Union of South Africa from the Commonwealth in 1961 ended another dream but opened few hopes for the future. The South Africa Act, 1909, had been introduced by a Liberal government to make a generous settlement between the British and the Afrikaners after the Boer war which the British had won with great difficulty. It was hoped that the two white communities in South Africa would henceforth work amicably together to build a prosperous state. It may have been hoped also that the British South African community would be the larger. Lord Milner and Cecil Rhodes certainly had a vision of a British-dominated South Africa. But ultimately the Afrikaners prevailed. The explosion which forced South Africa out of the Commonwealth was caused by three factors: the failure of British governments to stimulate emigration to South Africa; the cohesion of the Afrikaners in a fixed belief, upheld with Old Testament rigidity, in their mission to rule; and the rapid growth of Indian and African nationalism. South Africa has natural wealth, especially in her gold mines, and cheap African labour. On this basis the Afrikaners have built a state in which the white minority, defended by wealth and military power, could also be protected by social and political separation from the coloured majority—by apartheid. Since 1945 African nationalism has gained independence from white minorities in many parts of Africa, and this freedom has made the treatment of coloured people in South Africa more intolerable, not only to those who suffer from the policy of apartheid, but to a great body of opinion in the world outside. The Afro-Asian group in the United Nations has had the means to test international opinion on the question of racial segregation.

No British government which had supported the post-war development of the Commonwealth could have endorsed the policy of apartheid. At the end of 1959, Harold Macmillan travelled through Africa from Ghana to Nigeria (both of which are now independent African states), to Central and South Africa. In Cape Town, on February 3, 1960, he warned the South African Parliament that "the wind of change is blowing through this continent and, whether we like it or not, this growth of national consciousness is a political fact". Macmillan stated that Britain desired to give South Africa support and encouragement, but that "there are some aspects of your policies which make it impossible for us to do this without being false to our own deep convictions about the political destinies of free men to which, in our own territories, we are trying to give effect."

But while this had to be the basic position of the British Prime Minister, so long as the Commonwealth cohered, his government did not wish to drive South Africa out of the Commonwealth. It would have preferred South Africa to remain a member on condition that other members of the Commonwealth were free to express their detestation of apartheid. The South African government, under Dr Verwoerd's leadership, would not accept such terms, and decided to withdraw. The issue came to a head at the Commonwealth Prime Ministers' conference which met in London in March 1961. In the previous year the South African electorate had voted in favour of republican status in a plebiscite, but the Verwoerd government intended nevertheless to apply for continued membership of the Commonwealth. In the ordinary course this would certainly have been approved by other Commonwealth governments. The London conference had to consider this application. A formula was prepared, but never published, which would have approved of South Africa's application but expressed disapproval of apartheid. The tone of the conference was such, however, that South Africa found it unacceptable, and the new republic left the Commonwealth. As a result, a South Africa Act was passed in the British Parliament in 1962 which in effect provided that South Africa should henceforth be treated as any other friendly nation outside the Commonwealth. Special provisions were made to maintain Commonwealth trade preferences and to preserve military arrangements, particularly the facilities for the Royal Navy at Simonstown.

Labour and Liberal opinion in Britain could not regard South Africa, as her racial policies developed, as any other friendly nation. They demanded in 1963 that Britain should ban the export to South Africa of arms that might be used to enforce apartheid. Later in 1963 the South African government itself began to test the nerve of the British government by its suggestion that it should take over the administration of the three British Protectorates in South Africa, and by its efforts to stop the flight of African refugees from one Protectorate to another.

The British government's attitude to apartheid, and its acceptance of South Africa's withdrawal from the Commonwealth, made the possibility of establishing a multiracial federation in Central Africa much more difficult. The Federation of Rhodesia and Nyasaland had been formed in 1953 out of three unequal partners. It never took root; and in June 1963, representatives of the five governments concerned—those of the Federation, Britain, Southern Rhodesia, Northern Rhodesia and Nyasaland— met at Victoria Falls to arrange for its orderly winding up. It had virtually come to an end when the British minister responsible for Central African affairs, R. A. Butler, announced in December 1962 that the British government accepted in principle that Nyasaland should be allowed to withdraw.

The main cause of the instability of the Federation was the fear of the Africans that their interests would be subordinated to those of the white minority which controlled the governments of Southern Rhodesia and of the Federation itself. The dominant figure was the Federal Prime Minister, Sir Roy Welensky, who had formerly been Prime Minister of Southern Rhodesia. This was the most advanced of the three territories, largely as a result of investment and settlement by people of European stock. Northern Rhodesia, with its mineral deposits, was a valuable partner of Southern Rhodesia but had not attracted so many white settlers. Nyasaland, the poorest of the three, had been less attractive still as a country of European settlement. Advocates of the Federation believed that the three territories could work together to produce a multiracial group which might become an example of a new type of society in Africa. But its success depended on the establishment of self-government for the African majorities in Northern Rhodesia and Nyasaland. The Africans in those countries would have accepted nothing less, and without their assent, the British government was limited in the constitutional action it could take. By the end of 1963 both countries had complete self-government in sight.

This stimulated a demand from the government of Southern Rhodesia for complete independence, too, and on its own terms. Southern Rhodesia had long occupied a special status within the Commonwealth. Although not completely independent, her Prime Ministers attended meetings of Commonwealth Prime Ministers. The Labour and Liberal parties were unwilling that the British government should finally surrender all responsibility for Southern Rhodesia (however formal it might have been) until the rights of the Africans in Southern Rhodesia had been enlarged; and the government itself could not ignore this argument.

Central Africa presented Britain with a series of most difficult decisions; no government, of whatever party, could have found easy answers. As one country after another in Africa advanced to independence under majority rule, the demands of the Africans in Northern Rhodesia and Nyasaland became clamant; and the advances they made threw a harsher light on the position of Africans in Southern Rhodesia. But could any British government ignore the interests and achievements of the white minority in Southern Rhodesia? The whites themselves firmly believed that the British government had undertaken in 1953 to make no fundamental change in the Federation for at least ten years, and then only with the approval of the governments concerned. Lord Swinton and Lord Chandos, who had both been involved as British ministers in the negotiations of 1953, denied ten years later that any such pledge had been given. Apart from that, however, there was a genuine conflict of interest between the white rulers and developers of Southern Rhodesia and the African majority which it would have taken a government of saints or wizards to resolve to the satisfaction of both sides. A commission led by Lord Monckton in 1960, which surveyed the constitutional prospects for the Federation, found that some of the Federal and Southern Rhodesian legislation affecting the Africans was repressive and should be altered. It is possible that if these two governments had been more imaginative, and if successive Conservative governments in Britain had not been so careful to let the Federation run its own affairs, a situation might have developed which would have been more favourable to its continuance. British policy was unquestionably hampered by the division of responsibility between the Commonwealth Relations Office, which dealt on Commonwealth terms with the Federal and Southern Rhodesian governments, and the Colonial Office, which had the duty of safeguarding the protectorate status of Northern Rhodesia and Nyasaland. The transfer of the British government's responsibility for all three territories to a separate department had become essential if anything was to be saved from the wreck, but this change took place very late in the day.

Changes have been rapid in other parts of the world. A pattern of change has often repeated itself. The leader of a nationalist movement, anxious to advance quicker than the British government thought prudent, would be arrested for subversion. After a period in gaol he would return to his country to lead a new nationalist government. The histories of Archbishop Makarios in Cyprus, Kwame Nkrumah in Ghana and of Dr Banda in Nyasaland illustrate the process.

Malaya became independent in 1957, and Singapore was accorded full internal self-government. In September 1963, Malaya and Singapore, with North Borneo and Sarawak, joined in a Federation of Malaysia which was born in an atmosphere of turbulent protest from Indonesia.

In the West Indies, a detailed plan for federation collapsed in 1962, but Jamaica and Trinidad each became independent. The governments of a group of East Caribbean islands proposed in May 1963 that they should form a federation of their own. Political divisions and economic difficulties have hindered steady constitutional advance in British Guiana and have baffled successive British governments.

Although Cyprus became independent, Britain has not yet completed a scheme that satisfies the political parties in Malta. The British government intended that Malta should become independent in 1964. Gibraltar remains British. Aden is troubled by the restlessness of Arabs in neighbouring states.

All Commonwealth activities have been surveyed periodically by meetings of Commonwealth prime ministers and finance ministers. No Commonwealth organisation has ever been given power to impose any decision on any of the member states, but an economic consultative committee was set up for an exchange of proposals and ideas. By the end of 1963 it seemed that nothing less than an expansion of world trade would meet the needs of the Commonwealth as a whole. Britain, though continuing financial aid to under-developed countries, had not been able to put the economy of the West Indies, for example, on a stable base. One result of this was to create the conditions in which the British government introduced the Commonwealth Immigrants Bill in 1961 and ended, for the time being, the free entry into Britain of Commonwealth citizens. Immigrants from the West Indies were attracted to Britain by the better economic conditions, and, together with immigrants from India and Pakistan, accentuated the housing shortage in the larger British cities and brought a distinctive social element into urban life. Some colour prejudice was stirred up and proved fertile ground for the activities of fascist groups. The Commonwealth Immigrants Act, which many Conservatives had demanded of the government, controlled the inflow. Labour officially condemned the legislation and claimed that the problem of absorbing immigrants into British life should have been tackled from the social end, by increasing more rapidly the accommodation available, and by more intelligent social management. The Liberal Party Assembly at Brighton in September 1963 rejected a proposal for the repeal of the Act, but favoured a Commonwealth conference at which all the problems of migration might be settled by agreement. The Act was renewed for twelve months at the end of 1963.

The economic future of the Commonwealth as a unit formed a large part of the argument among the political parties in Britain during the negotiations for Britain's entry into the European Economic Community, and has continued to be debated since the negotiations failed. Supporters both of the Conservative and Labour parties maintained that Commonwealth development was more promising than Britain's entry into Europe on terms which might hinder Commonwealth trade. Advocates of Britain's entry claimed that this would open valuable new markets to Commonwealth exporters and would be a stage in the expansion of world trade. It is profitless now to attempt a balance sheet of the operation, but the argument revealed agreement on one development: the search for world commodity agreements from which the Commonwealth stood to benefit.

VIII

BRITAIN'S FUTURE

1. INTERNATIONAL PROSPECT

The British need not fear the future if they look squarely at the present and see from it where they have to go. National pride need not be injured or destroyed if its virtues are directed into new channels. The British have now to establish new relations with the people of other countries, not only traditional friends or enemies, but new nations, new groupings. The old international pattern has been broken and if Britain is to have a proper place in the new pattern that is emerging she must adjust many of her domestic and overseas policies. The British have been varying their social and political relations for centuries: the process must now be controlled by a conscious effort to recognise the shifts in power that have occurred since 1945 and are still taking place.

Britain's national strength lies in her people's inventiveness, administrative ability, physical courage, inquiring concern, endurance and tolerance. Sometimes the British are seers but mostly they are doers with a capacity to take each day as it comes without fretting about the day after. This capacity will be especially needed if Britain is to apply the changes which the future will impose on her. The British have not yet lost their national characteristics which can be put eagerly to new uses if the record of the past is truly appreciated. Old glories are dangerous only if they are a refuge from the present and the future. The story of the East India Company and later of the Indian Civil Service should support the nation's readiness to accept responsibility in new fields. The practice of the East India Company in placing heavy duties on mere boys, fresh from England and with no experience of affairs whatever, seems in retrospect to have been almost frivolous, but by and large the system worked. The boys soon learned to govern. The new world will not offer the material gains that were to be picked up in eighteenth century India but it will find places for men of administrative ability. The British act on the assumption, perhaps more readily than they should, that almost any task can be given to a fellow countryman with a reasonable chance that it will be tolerably well done. The army carried this rule to ridiculous lengths during the war. It might order a junior NCO, for example, to produce, as a military duty, a BBC programme running for three-quarters of an hour. Once the order had been given, the NCO would in theory have been liable to a charge of neglecting his military duty if the programme had been a failure.

Physical courage, even assertiveness, are still needed. They might be useful one day to a world government. It is a question of finding the right outlet for them. Does the born fighter fight only for his country, or for the sake of fighting, or because the conditions in which he is allowed to fight suit his temperament and his opinions? The history of mercenaries, of ideological campaigners—on both sides in the Spanish Civil War, for instance—and of United Nations troops in the Congo shows that national causes are not the only means of using this kind of energy.

It is, in any case, already evident that the acceptance of international obligations has brought gains to Britain even if it has also caused political irritation. The standard of living has risen steadily since 1945. In September 1963 the Chancellor of the Exchequer, Reginald Maudling, described Britain's trade figures for the previous month as excellent. The value of British exports in August of that year was £351 million: the highest ever recorded in one month. In the same month the value of imports into Britain had dropped from £419 million in July to £398 million and the deficit on the import-export account had fallen from £66 million in July to £34 million. Although there has been much criticism of Conservative governments by the Labour and Liberal parties for failing to secure a larger increase in the rate of growth of Britain's national income, and for failing to secure a larger investment in industry, there has, nevertheless, been a massive social and industrial investment in Britain since 1945. In 1962-63 the small savings of individuals produced a net increase of £180 million for national investment. There were many visible signs of increased prosperity since the war. The output of the car industry was higher in May 1963, at 35,000 vehicles a week, than ever before. Much of this output is exported, but the ownership of cars in Britain has increased at a rate that has made traffic congestion in the cities a grave social problem. Parking meters have had to be introduced in an attempt to ease the blockage. In the new towns, planned as balanced communities to limit the growth of large cities, the authorities find a constant need to increase the proportion of garages to houses.

Large changes in commercial and financial practice were being considered in 1963. On September 23, the government published a report (Cmnd. 2145) from a committee presided over by Lord Halsbury on the feasibility of introducing a system of decimal coinage in Britain. In the same month, the government published a report from an Anglo-French committee of experts which had examined proposals for improving cross-Channel facilities. The committee found in favour of a tunnel and rejected the scheme for a bridge. The government asked for the comments of the public before coming to a decision.

Changes in the nature of Britain's industrial output have been taking place for many years but were accelerated in the decade ending in 1963. The government made some effort to meet the social and economic consequences of this shift. In particular, the National Coal Board, in its plans to develop economic mines and to close those which were becoming worked out, took unusual care—unusual, that is, in British industrial history—to effect the changes with the least hardship to the miners it employed. In general, Britain's energy has been steadily diverted from the traditional heavy industries of coal, ship-building and locomotive engineering, into the development of electrical goods, electronics, plastics, communications, oil and nuclear energy.

The wider and deeper international commitments which Britain might feel obliged to accept in the future could open a new prospect of change and development. The economic and defence system of the United States might itself be turned into a fuller partnership. The need for Britain to be ready to promote such a change was the theme of a pamphlet on *Atlantic Community* by six Conservatives (led by Lady Elliot of Harwood) published by the Conservative Political Centre in September 1963. They urged Britain to step out of the "twilight of nationalism" and to cultivate a "Community" sense. They argued that the Western allies might be in a better position to deal with the communist group if the West became a real community: political as well as economic and military.

The most tantalising prospect of all, however, was the possibility of easier relations with the Soviet Union and her satellite states east of the Iron Curtain. If the Soviet Union, as a result of its quarrel with Communist China, became more willing to talk and do business with the West, the situation in Europe could be transformed. Any acceptable reduction in the military forces which meet each other in Germany would not only strengthen world security but be of unqualified benefit to a Britain which finds it so expensive to maintain her overseas garrisons. Added to this would be the benefit of a real increase at least in East-West trade. Hitherto, the Soviet government has been unwilling to find the foreign exchange for the import of consumer goods; it has preferred to import the machinery to make them. Yet the people of the communist states mostly endure under a standard of life below that of the people in the West, in spite of the fact that since the war the Soviet economy has developed rapidly under a strict system of priorities. In 1963 Russia was exporting machine tools. Granted a period of reduced tension between East and West, the Soviet economy could certainly make still greater advances and increase the purchasing power of the communist states. If that were to happen, the movement towards larger economic groupings and freer world trade which was evident in the West in the 1960s might be speeded.

Nowhere would the effects of such a change be more apparent than in Germany, an economic giant cut into two separate units by the mutual distrust of the Soviet and Western power systems. An easing of East-West relations which led to the creation of a zone of controlled disarmament in Germany and in neighbouring states to the East could conceivably lead to German reunification in conditions that would alarm no one and could bring Berlin back into its traditional life as a capital city. The Labour Party and perhaps a number of Conservatives would welcome some accommodation between East and West Germany as a means of circumnavigating the awkward problems of West German control of nuclear weapons. Liberals would welcome it, too, provided that freer conditions were also created for individuals in the satellite states. The Liberal Party, with its insistence on respect for individuals, has been particularly sensitive about the effects of communist authoritarianism. It would be foolish, however, to suppose that the division of Europe could easily be ended. The stopping of American and British convoys by communist troops in Germany in October and November 1963 was a reminder of the obstacles that have still to be overcome.

The price to Britain of fitting more closely into a Western grouping and into an East-West détente would be not only a further loss of sovereignty but an inevitable trend towards a more thorough planning of her own economy. This would compel all parties to extend the studies, initiated by the Liberals, of how to give the individual a feeling that he has a real part to play in the life and work of the country. Would it be a condition of European unity, of East-West co-operation, that all the nations concerned should become more centralised? The trend was quite plain by 1963.

In Britain, the steady concentration of industry into large units has accelerated rapidly and swept up concerns—brewing, for instance—which were not obviously dependent on the heavy capital outlay and maintenance costs needed by the chemical and man-made fibre industries. Pressure has been increased (against the wishes of the trade unions themselves) for the regrouping of workers in industrial instead of craft unions. The political development of Western Europe seems likely to foster state control. What kind of régime will follow that of President de Gaulle in France? What would be the effect on the West German economy if the Social Democrats won power? How soon will the growing vigour of the communists in Italy make a strong political impact? If the communist system were generally to become more flexible, as it had already become in Poland and Yugoslavia, might this not influence the conduct of non-communist states?

The first need for Britain, if she is to find her proper place in the world, is to discover clear objectives, make them perfectly intelligible to the people and get them accepted as reasonable by the majority. Radical alterations in a nation's economic and social life only last if they are based on common consent. Individuals will have to allow more consciously for each other's well-being. The lawyer, for instance, comfortable in his private professional world, must imagine what it is like to be, say, a pattern maker who has to change his job and home. By 1963, the government had begun tentatively to undertake some social planning, but it seems certain that the work will have to be greatly expanded in the future.

It may prove even more difficult for Britain, with her long tradition of overseas rule, to accept the new nations with which she will have to work. The activities of the Afro-Asian group in the United Nations and the emergence of a colour problem in Britain have already been noted. The British do not resent the belated arrival of the Africans on the world scene but it is too recent to have become an accepted fact of life. (Some of the British have scarcely accepted Egypt as a nation yet.) Political education, conducted by the Conservative Party among others, and the campaigns of societies formed to promote better understanding between coloured and white people, have worked since the war to lessen the shock which the birth of African nations was bound to create. But the establishment since 1945 of a large coloured community in Britain has caused some social unrest—on the whole, not so much as might have been expected—and directly confronted the British, for the first time in their history, with the need to take immediate account of the existence of millions of coloured people with all the demands of human beings and all the hopes of free men. The world in which the British travelled on privilege tickets as rich milords or rulers has gone for ever. This loss has its inconveniences but it has gains as well: the other travellers can be amusing, stimulating, instructive. If the British must now travel with coloured people as equal citizens they may also get to know their fellow-whites better. British policy will not suffer if it is based on thorough knowledge of other people. Such knowledge might have prevented a British government from supposing that President Nasser could easily be toppled out of power in Egypt. It might have saved Britain from making woeful miscalculations about the hold of Hitler on nazi Germany.

2. THE ELECTORS' JUDGMENT

In 1964 the British electors will have to decide which of the parties they regard as best equipped to find the country's track through this changing world. In September and October 1963 the Liberal, Labour and Conservative parties held the last of their annual conferences before the election. Each party aimed to deploy its troops in the most challenging position. The Conservatives' issue of battle orders was interrupted by the news of the illness of the Prime Minister, Harold Macmillan, and of his intention to resign. The Conservative Party Conference was held at Blackpool from October 9 to 12. On October 8 it was announced that the Prime Minister had entered hospital for an operation. On October 10 he stated that he could not lead the party at the next election and that he hoped a new leader would be found through "the customary processes of consultation". On October 18 Macmillan resigned the office of Prime Minister and advised the Queen to invite Lord Home, the Foreign Secretary, to form a new government. On October 19 Lord Home, sure by then that he could do so, was appointed Prime Minister. The new cabinet was completed on the following day. Since 1902 the Prime Minister has always been a member of the House of Commons, and to continue this practice Lord Home disclaimed his peerage under the terms of the Peerage Act 1963 and contested the Kinross and West Perth by-election as Sir Alexander Douglas-Home. The timetable of the by-election made it impossible that the new Prime Minister could be a member of the House of Commons by October 29, the date originally fixed by Macmillan's government for the opening of the last session of the Parliament elected in 1959. He therefore decided, despite the official protest of the leader of the opposition, Harold Wilson, to defer the opening of the new session until November 12: four days after the result of the by-election had been declared.

The struggle for the leadership of the Conservative Party was open and intense. There seemed at first to be three contestants: R. A. Butler, Lord Hailsham and Reginald Maudling. Lord Home never declared himself to be in the fight but he was believed to be available if the party could not agree on one of the other three. Butler was Deputy Prime Minister, First Secretary of State and the minister responsible for Central African affairs. He had been a candidate for the leadership in 1957 when Sir Anthony Eden resigned and Harold Macmillan was chosen. Hailsham was Lord President of the Council, Minister for Science, and leader of the House of Lords. He announced on October 10 that he would disclaim his peerage and seek a seat in the House of Commons. On December 5, as Quintin Hogg, he was elected as member for St Marylebone. Maudling was Chancellor of the Exchequer.

Public attention was fixed on the personalities in this struggle between three claimants representing different elements in the Conservative Party. Butler had great experience of office and was a moderating influence. Hailsham was regarded as the most powerful propagandist for the party but with uncertain judgment and a tendency to jingoism. Maudling was the choice of the younger men who wished their party to give firm support to new technological and commercial ventures, and to show itself as belonging to the new industrial age rather than to the old aristocratic tradition. Opinion in the cabinet, among Conservative members of Parliament and among party workers in the constituencies, was split on the merits of these three, none of whom was ready, until too late in the contest, to withdraw his own claims in favour of those of any other candidate. Thus, when Macmillan decided to advise the Queen to send for Lord Home it was claimed that Home commanded the greatest measure of support in the party. This claim was disputed by other Conservatives, and two members of Macmillan's cabinet, Iain Macleod, who had been leader of the House of Commons and joint chairman of the Conservative Party Organisation, and Enoch Powell, who had been Minister of Health, refused to serve in the Douglas-Home government. Butler took office as Foreign Secretary, Hailsham agreed to continue as Lord President of the Council and Minister for Science, and Maudling agreed to remain Chancellor of the Exchequer.

The public effect of this extraordinarily bitter struggle was to prove the existence of animosities which had been concealed so long as Macmillan was Prime Minister. The outcome of the struggle left open the question whether a party led by an aristocrat, even though he had disclaimed his peerage, would appeal to the electors as well fitted to manage the technological revolution taking place in Britain. One of Sir Alec's first acts was to

state in a broadcast that his government had been con-
structed to concentrate attention on economic growth.
Edward Heath, formerly in charge of negotiations for
Britain's entry into the European Economic Community,
had been appointed to the new post of Secretary of State
for Industry, Trade and Regional Development, combined
with the duties of President of the Board of Trade. The
Ministers of Power and of Public Buildings and Works
had been brought into the cabinet. Sir Alec claimed that
these changes would give new impetus to the economy of
the country.

The new Prime Minister, during the period when, as
Minister of State for Scotland, he had economic and
social responsibilities, made no mark in this field of
policy; but in foreign affairs he represented the common
mind of the Conservative Party better than almost anyone else. At the Blackpool Conference, which he addressed as Foreign Secretary, and in his broadcasts as
Prime Minister, he made clear what the Conservative
appeal to the electors on foreign policy would be. His
government, like Macmillan's, believed that Britain's
retention of an independent nuclear deterrent was the
only guarantee that Britain would continue to share with
the United States and the Soviet Union in discussion at
the highest level. He based British foreign policy solidly
on the Atlantic alliance and warned his party against
"Little Englanders". In one of his broadcasts he was questioned about his attitude to the United Nations and to the
Afro-Asian group. He was more guarded in his reply than
he had been in his speech at Berwick-on-Tweed, but
claimed that the Afro-Asian group knew that Britain was
"decolonising" as quickly as it could safely be done, and
that it was unreasonable to attack Britain for her colonial
policy.

The Liberal Assembly (Brighton, September 11-14)
and the Labour Party Conference (Scarborough, Septem-

ber 30-October 4) both took place before Macmillan had announced his retirement. Liberal and Labour delegates alike, however, tried to get their respective policies into election trim, and did so with an idea of the broad lines of the attack which the Conservatives would launch against them. Sir Alec's appointment as Prime Minister did not lead Labour and the Liberals substantially to alter their assessments of the Conservatives' position.

The Conservatives at Blackpool were reminded over and over again by ministers that the Labour conference had not debated foreign policy or defence. The Liberal Assembly did not debate them directly, either. Both the Labour and the Liberal parties had debated these two subjects in the immediate past and their policies have already been mentioned in this book. Nevertheless, the Conservatives determined to ram home at the general election this omission from their rivals' 1963 conferences. The Conservatives counted on gaining the total "patriotic" vote for their policy of maintaining an independent British deterrent.

It seemed most likely, however, that the election would be fought on domestic issues—employment, housing, education, health, transport, pensions—and these topics occupied the greater part of the time of all three conferences. Housing was recognised by all as the most urgent social issue. The Liberal Assembly rejected a proposal for a target of 500,000 new houses a year as unattainable but it adopted a target of 375,000 a year. The Conservatives also rejected a proposal for 500,000 a year, but supported Sir Keith Joseph, the Minister of Housing and Local Government, when he said that it should be possible to build 400,000 a year for the five years after 1965. Labour adopted no target but accepted policies designed to bring down the cost of land and to reduce interest rates on housing loans. Labour's principal proposal was to set up a land commission which would buy the freehold of land on which building or rebuilding was to take place. This policy fell short of complete land nationalisation but was sharply attacked by the Conservative Conference on the grounds that it would be unjust to landowners and would reduce rather than increase the amount of land put on the market for urban development. The Liberals adopted a different means of reducing "the crippling price of land": a graduated tax on the difference between the previous capital value of a site and its actual selling price.

Alternative means of expanding the economy became a major theme for the election. The subject involved incomes policy, education and the use of scientific knowledge. Harold Wilson made this the topic of his first major speech as party leader to the Labour Conference, and the Conservatives were rather worried by his success. It was a direct appeal to scientists, technologists and to all who sought wider educational opportunities in Britain to support Labour's programme for still more universities, including a "University of the Air", and for a radical development of the state education system. The Labour Conference followed the example of the Liberal Assembly in rejecting a proposal for the abolition of the independent, fee-paying schools. The Liberals voted for a massive extension of higher education. The Conservative Conference was denied details of a higher education policy because the government was then awaiting the report of the Robbins committee, which was published on October 23, 1963. It proposed, as a matter of urgency, that six new universities in Britain should be started at once and that by 1980 the number of institutions of university status should be eighty compared with thirty-two to-day. The Robbins committee recommended that the number of full-time students receiving higher education should be raised from 216,000 in 1962-63 to 560,000 in 1980-81. The government at once accepted this rate

of expansion of higher education. This decision, taken
with those of the Liberal Assembly and the Labour Conference, meant that Britain would be committed under
any government to heavy expenditure on education in the
next twenty years. The Robbins proposals alone will involve a capital cost of £1,420 million. But education is
not the only social service that is to grow, whichever
party wins the next election. All parties, therefore, knew
it was imperative to increase the national wealth and to
recognise the conditions in which this could best be done.

Detailed policies adopted by the various parties
mattered less in electoral terms than the prevailing moods
of the parties themselves and of the voters generally.
Labour approached the election in better shape than it
had been at any time since it lost office in 1951. Wilson's
first conference as leader could not have helped him more.
He sought to by-pass the old nationalisation controversy
by applying practical tests to future needs. Trade union
leaders, Frank Cousins and Ted Hill, softened the impact
of the decision of the Trades Union Congress to resist a
policy of wage restraint by supporting, at the Labour
Conference, a policy of "the planned growth of wages".

The test for Labour in preparing for the election was
whether the party could make the voters enthusiastic
about Labour's policies as relevant to modern needs. The
Conservatives at Blackpool condemned Labour's policies
as cumbersome and restrictive, and drew a contrast between a socialist world of controls and shortages and a
capitalist world of plenty and free choice.

The Conservative Conference in 1963 did not provide a pre-election stimulus because it was overshadowed
by the search for a new leader. Moreover, the Conservatives met at Blackpool knowing that their party had been
losing the support of the electors for many months past.
Labour and the Liberals had united in condemning the

236

government's wage restraint policy as unfair, its foreign policy as confused—at Suez, in the approach to Europe, in the Congo and over the nuclear deterrent—and its management of national security as incompetent. The charge of incompetence was pressed following the publication, on September 26, 1963, of a report by Lord Denning, a High Court judge, on the security and other aspects of the circumstances which led to the resignation of J. D. Profumo, Secretary of State for War, on June 4, 1963.

Lord Denning found that security had not been broken by Profumo or any other minister, and that there was no basis for a mass of rumours linking the names of other ministers with those of Christine Keeler, with whom Profumo had had sexual relations, of the late Dr Stephen Ward, and of Captain Ivanov, a Soviet intelligence officer who had for a time been posted to London. Ward had sought information on Anglo-American relations for the Russians. He tried to find out whether Western Germany was to be given nuclear weapons and what action Britain would take at the height of the American-Soviet crisis over Cuba.

Lord Denning's findings settled the main security issue. (R. A. Butler dismissed the Profumo affair in a sentence at the Conservative Conference at Blackpool. The Labour Conference never debated the subject at all.) In setting out the facts of the case, however, Lord Denning described a series of incidents and administrative arrangements which led Labour and Liberals to claim that the government had bungled its control of security. Lord Denning stated that none of the existing security machinery provided a routine for the examination of the moral conduct of a minister. He stated that since 1952 the Home Secretary had been responsible for the security service. This came as a surprise, for most members of the House of Commons had assumed that the Prime Minister

237

held this responsibility, and indeed he had always himself answered questions on security. The impression that the Home Secretary's responsibility for security was generally unknown was deepened by Lord Denning's account of a meeting of five ministers, in the early hours of March 22, 1963, when Profumo was asked about charges which had just been made against him in the House of Commons. At this meeting a statement was drafted which Profumo made in the House of Commons later the same day, and in which he denied that he had had sexual relations with Christine Keeler. (He later admitted that he had lied on this occasion.) The Home Secretary, Henry Brooke, had been present in the House when charges were brought against Profumo but had gone home at the end of the debate. No minister thought it necessary to bring him back for the meeting with Profumo.

Macmillan replied to the accusation of incompetence arising out of the Denning report in a broadcast he made on the day of its publication. He said he had explained to the House on three occasions the division of responsibility for security between ministers. He defended the conduct of the five ministers who saw Profumo on March 22 on two grounds: first, that they did not believe that a security risk was involved and therefore had no reason to call in the Home Secretary; and secondly, that they were the victims of their trust in the word of their colleague who had assured them that he had had no sexual relations with Christine Keeler. The government, added Macmillan, deserved the sympathy of the public and not its censure: a minister seldom lied as Profumo had done.

The Profumo affair was only one of a number of incidents during the Conservatives' period of office which raised issues of security. The Conservatives pointed out that every security case which is made public is proof of the efficiency of the security service.

As an item in the election campaign, security seemed unlikely to be so prominent as domestic policy. The Conservatives' main appeal to the country was to support the development of existing policies and guard against the effects of Labour's programme. The Conservatives hoped that, as in 1951, 1955 and 1959, the electors would be too content with their present lot to risk any change.

The unknown quantity in the election plans of Conservatives and Labour was the effect of Liberal candidatures. The Liberal Assembly at Brighton met in an uneasy mood. Delegates had expected their party to win one or two more by-elections during the year. The chief duty of the Liberal leader, Jo Grimond, when he addressed the Assembly, was to keep his party steady by giving it a realistic estimate of the rate of progress it might achieve, and by reassuring them of the relevance of the Liberal purpose to secure social reform without socialism. He warned the over-optimistic not to expect a Liberal government to emerge from the forthcoming election. "If we return after the election with a solid block of Liberals in the House of Commons, even if we do not hold a majority," he said, "we shall be able to influence the whole thinking of the country and the attitude of whatever party may be in power."

Grimond heartened his party; but as the election approached, the reward which the voters would give it remained uncertain. The issue lay between the success of Labour in presenting itself as a party of new vigour and the success of the Conservative Party in convincing the public that it had regained its old momentum.

CHAPTER I

A PERIOD OF CHANGE

1. Anthony Hartley, *A State of England*, Hutchinson, London, 1963, pp. 58-9.
2. Text released by Foreign Office, London, April 9, 1963.
3. Anthony Hartley, *op. cit.*, p. 60.
4. Prime Minister January 1957 to October 1963.
5. Conservative Party's official report, London, 1962, p. 147.
6. *Ibid.*, pp. 148 and 149.

CHAPTER II

LABOUR GAINS POWER

1. Winston S. Churchill, *The Second World War*, Vol. II, Cassell, London, 1949, pp. 8 and 9; Houghton Mifflin, Boston.
2. *Ibid*, p. 439.
3. Lord Beaverbrook, *Men and Power*, Hutchinson, London, 1956; Meredith, New York, 1957.
4. Lord Beaverbrook, *The Decline and Fall of Lloyd George*, Collins, London, 1963; Meredith, New York, 1963.
5. Harry Boardman, *The Glory of Parliament*, George Allen and Unwin, London, 1960, p. 92; Taplinger, New York, 1957.
6. Lord Beveridge, *Power and Influence*, Hodder and Stoughton, London, 1953, p. 316; Houghton Mifflin, Boston.
7. Winston S. Churchill, *The Second World War*, Vol. IV, Cassell, London, 1951, pp. 861–2; Houghton Mifflin, Boston.
8. Lord Beveridge, *op. cit.*, p. 332.
9. Lord Morrison of Lambeth, *Herbert Morrison, An Autobiography*, Odhams, London, 1960, p. 166.

CHAPTER III

THE PARLIAMENTARY SYSTEM

1. John Morley, *Life of Gladstone*, Vol. III, Macmillan, London, 1903, p. 377.

CHAPTER IV

THE POLITICAL PARTIES

1. Henry James, *The Portrait of a Lady* (1881), Penguin Books edition, London, 1963, p. 56.
2. Andrew Roth, *The Business Background of Members of Parliament*, Parliamentary Profiles, London, 1963 edition, p. xvi.
3. Selwyn Lloyd was dismissed from the Macmillan government in July 1962. He entered the Douglas-Home government as Lord Privy Seal and leader of the House of Commons in October 1963.
4. *Hansard*, April 17, 1961, column 820.
5. *Hansard*, April 20, 1961, columns 1516-7.
6. Emanuel Shinwell, *The Labour Story*, Macdonald, London, 1963, p. 98.
7. Henry Pelling, *A Short History of the Labour Party*, Macmillan, London, 1961, p. 45; St Martins, New York, 1961.
8. *Op. cit.*, p. 9.
9. C. A. R. Crosland, *The Future of Socialism*, Cape, London, 1956, p. 87; rev. ed., Schocken, New York, 1963, p. 51.
10. Jo Grimond, *In Praise of Politics*, Students' Representative Council, Edinburgh, 1961, p. 6.

CHAPTER V

MONEY

1. Hugh Dalton, *Memoirs 1945-1960, High Tide and After*, Frederick Muller, London, 1962.

CHAPTER VI

TRADE AND INDUSTRY

1. A shift of trade unionists' attitude to a wages policy is mentioned in Chapter VIII.
2. *Hansard*, February 12, 1959, column 1381.

CHAPTER VII

DEFENCE AND OVERSEAS POLICY

1. Conservative Central Office, London, 1949, p. 289.
2. In October 1963 Butler became Foreign Secretary in the Douglas-Home government and responsibility for Central African affairs went to Sandys.

INDEX